The Hand-Stitched Flower Garden

The Hand-Stitched Flower Garden

Over 45 beautiful floral designs to embroider,

plus 20 great project ideas

YUKI SUGASHIMA

KODANSHA

A QUARTO BOOK

First published in North America in 2015 by
Kodansha USA, Inc.
451 Park Avenue South
New York, NY 10016
www.kodanshausa.com

Library of Congress Cataloging-in-
Publication Data
Sugashima, Yuki.
    The hand-stitched flower garden : 40
beautiful floral designs to embroider, plus
20 great project ideas / by Yuki
Sugashima.
    pages cm
    "A Quarto book."
ISBN 978-1-56836-566-4 (paperback)
1. Embroidery--Patterns. 2. Decoration
and ornament--Plant forms. I. Title.
    TT773.S795 2015
    746.44--dc23
                2015023882

Conceived, designed, and produced by
Quarto Publishing plc
The Old Brewery
6 Blundell Street
London
N7 9BH

QUA: EFLC

Senior editor: Chelsea Edwards
Copyeditor: Claire Waite Brown
Art editor and designer: Jackie Palmer
Photography: Nicki Dowey (location)
    Phil Wilkins (studio)
Illustrator: John Woodcock
Proofreader: Corinne Masciocchi
Indexer: Helen Snaith
Art director: Caroline Guest

Creative director: Moira Clinch
Publisher: Paul Carslake

Color separation by PICA Digital Pte Ltd,
Singapore
Printed by 1010 Printing International Ltd,
China

Contents

Welcome to Yuki's world   6

Welcome to Yuki's world

It was when I discovered a forgotten box of floss at the back of the closet that I decided to give embroidery a try. Buried among all my old craft supplies, it had been lingering there since grade school when making friendship bracelets was the craze. Still neatly wound on thread cards and arranged in a rainbow, the floss awakened my interest in a craft that I thought I'd someday like to try… It turned out, that day was my "someday."

Up until that time, I had been an avid knitter, spinner, and natural dyer on a quest to create from sheep to shawl, but that was soon replaced by my newfound interest. I started with a sampler, then got a few books from the library to learn more. From the beginning, I wanted to stitch my own designs and discovered that even the simplest of drawings can gain depth and beauty by expressing it in stitches. My previous experience as a floral designer instilled in me a passion for flowers, and I was soon creating floral motifs and arrangements, this time, in thread.

Embroidery is a very accessible craft with numerous avenues to explore. Starting with just a few basic stitches, it's possible to create pretty motifs, and adding a little embroidery to everyday items can make them unique and a joy to use. If you've ever thought that you'd like to try embroidery, I hope this book will inspire you to take the first stitch and make this your "someday" too.

About this book

This book offers a selection of nature-inspired embroidery designs for making projects that reflect every season. Each section begins by displaying the motifs of the season, followed by imaginative projects that incorporate these design elements. At the end of the book is a collection of useful tools, techniques, and templates to help you create beautiful embroidery at any time of the year.

A YEAR IN STITCHES
Each section begins with a colorful spread of embroidery flora and fauna which reflect the nature of each season.

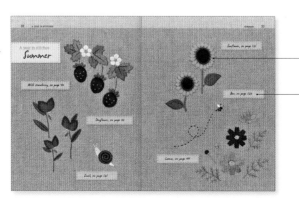

Beautiful photographs of the finished, delicate motif

Page numbers direct you to the appropriate page where you can find out how to stitch the motif

PROJECTS

These 20 creative projects will allow you to showcase your new motifs.

Color palette for easy identification of the shades you'll be using

Materials section complete with exact measurements required to create the project

The number for the DMC thread you need will be given here, along with the number of strands required in brackets.

The completed embroidery project

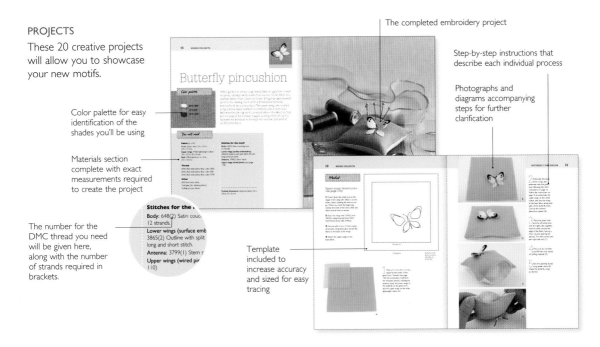

Step-by-step instructions that describe each individual process

Photographs and diagrams accompanying steps for further clarification

Template included to increase accuracy and sized for easy tracing

STITCH DIRECTORY

Each of the stitches used in the motifs is clearly shown in this section.

Instructions that break down stitching into simple, easy-to-follow steps

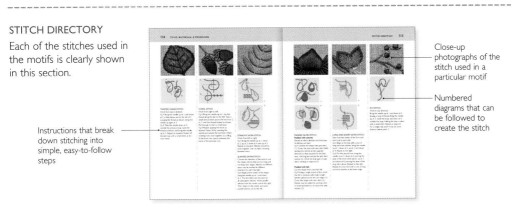

Close-up photographs of the stitch used in a particular motif

Numbered diagrams that can be followed to create the stitch

TEMPLATES

Here each motif that is not included on a project is featured at actual size for you to trace off.

Stitches used for each portion of the motif is included

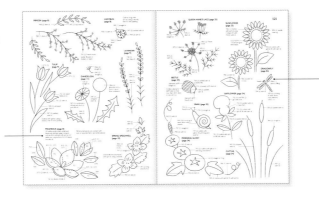

The DMC thread number is given as well as the number of strands required

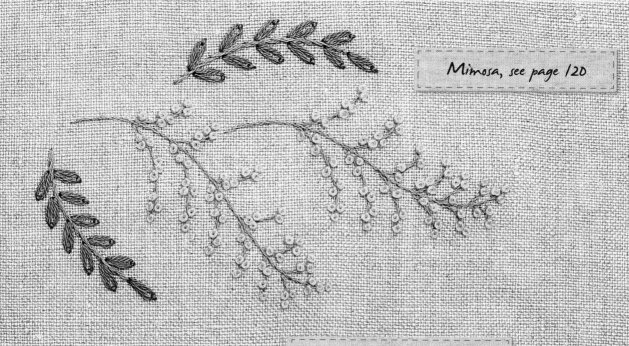

Mimosa, see page 120

A year in stitches
Spring

Ladybug, see page 120

Magnolia, see page 120

Tulip, see page 120

Lavender, see page 120

Spring snowflakes, see page 22

Daffodil, see page 24

Red clover, see page 28

Spring speedwell, see page 120

Butterfly, see page 16

Dandelion, see page 120

Violets, see page 12

Violet sewing machine cover

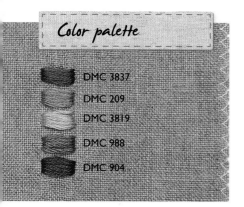
Making your own cover for the sewing machine is a great way to give your crafting space a fresh makeover and, at the same time, keep your machine dust free. The boxy shape is simple to construct with only a few straight seams to sew, and can accommodate sewing machines of various shapes. Strengthening the fabric with interfacing means the cover is crisp, sturdy, and holds its shape well. The violet motif offers a lovely opportunity for stitching color variations, so choose a combination that complements the gingham or the accent fabric of your choice.

You will need

Fabric (L x W)

Exterior main: Beige heather cotton/linen blend, 25½ x 24 in. (65 x 61 cm)

Exterior contrast: Purple gingham cotton/linen blend, two pieces measuring 4¼ x 24 in. (11 x 61 cm)

Interfacing: Iron-on interfacing, one piece measuring 24¾ x 24 in. (63 x 61 cm) and two pieces measuring 3⅛ x 24 in. (8 x 61 cm)

Thread

DMC #25 embroidery floss, color 3837
DMC #25 embroidery floss, color 209
DMC #25 embroidery floss, color 3819
DMC #25 embroidery floss, color 988
DMC #25 embroidery floss, color 904

Stitches for the motif

Flower: 209(2) Outline with split stitch along the top edge of each petal, fill with long and short stitch. Switch to 3837(2) closer to the center, as shown.

Flower center: 3819(2) French knots.

Stem: 988(2) Wrapped stem stitch.

Leaves: 904(2) Split stitch outline, padded satin stitch (one layer).

Finished dimensions:
Approximately 15¾ in. (40 cm) long, 7½ in. (19 cm) wide, and 12 in. (30 cm) tall

Violet motif
at actual size

Method

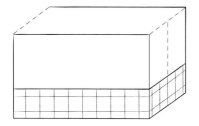

Final constructed piece

1 Attach interfacing to the fabric pieces. The width of the interfacing should align with the width of the fabrics. For the main fabric, the length of the interfacing should be ⅜ in. (1 cm) from the fabric edge on both ends; for the contrast fabrics, the length should be ⅜ in. (1 cm) on the top edge and ¾ in. (2 cm) from the bottom edge (A).

2 Transfer the motif (see page 106) 1¼ in. (3.5 cm) from the bottom edge of the main fabric and center it width-wise (B). Embroider following the stitch instructions on page 12.

3 With right sides together, machine stitch the top edge of one of the contrast fabric pieces to the main fabric along one short end. Repeat for the other short end with the second piece of contrast fabric. Finish the fabric edges with zigzag stitch (C and D).

4 Fold the seam allowance toward the contrast fabric side, then machine stitch in place from the right side (E).

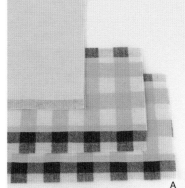

A

B

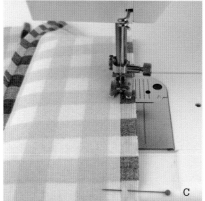

C

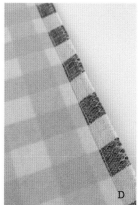

D

E

F

View of corner opened out flat

Open flat

Right sides together

Pressed side seam

Cutting line

⅜ in.
(1 cm)

7½ in.
(19 cm)

Sewing line

Wrong side of fabric

G

H

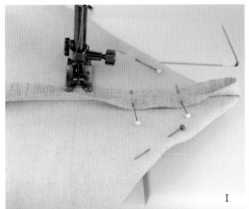

I

J

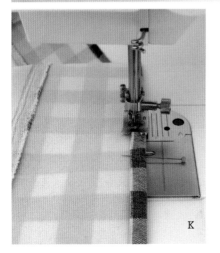

K

5 Fold widthwise with right sides together, and sew along both side edges (F and G). Press open the seams.

6 With the pressed side seam running down the center, flatten out the cover. It should result in a pointed end. Sew parallel to the point so that you form a triangle with a base that is 7½ in. (19 cm) wide (H and I).

7 Cut off the point about ⅜ in. (1 cm) above the stitching. Finish the edge with zigzag stitch. Repeat for the other side of the corner (J).

8 Along the bottom edge, fold half the width of the seam allowance toward the wrong side. Fold the same amount again, encasing the raw edge, and machine stitch in place (K). Turn the case right-side out.

Butterfly pincushion

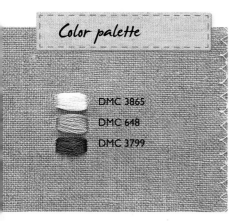

Color palette

DMC 3865

DMC 648

DMC 3799

When golden *nanohana* (rapeseed) blooms signal the arrival of spring, cabbage white butterflies are sure to be there too, playfully flitting from flower to flower. Bring that light-hearted spirit to the sewing room with a dimensional butterfly embroidered on a pincushion. The upper wings are created using a stumpwork method of outlining a form with wire before embroidering, so it can stand above the fabric surface and be shaped for a more realistic-looking effect. It's as if a butterfly has fluttered in through the window and settled on the pincushion.

You will need

Fabric (L x W)

Front: Green linen, 5½ x 5½ in. (14 x 14 cm)
Upper wings: White lightweight cotton, 3⅛ x 3⅛ in. (8 x 8 cm)
Back: Off-white linen, 4 x 4 in. (10 x 10 cm)

Thread

DMC #25 embroidery floss, color 3865
DMC #25 embroidery floss, color 648
DMC #25 embroidery floss, color 3799

Other

#30 floral wire, white
Craft glue (for adhering fabric)
Stuffing of your choice

Stitches for the motif

Body: 648(2) Satin couching over 12 strands.
Lower wings (surface embroidery): 3865(2) Outline with split stitch, fill with long and short stitch.
Antenna: 3799(1) Stem stitch.
Upper wings (wired piece): (see page 110)

Finished dimensions: Approximately 3⅛ x 3⅛ in. (8 x 8 cm)

Method

Upper wings (wired piece, see page 110):

1 Couch down the white wire in the shape of the wing with 3865(1) on the white cotton, bending the wire as you go. When you reach the beginning, overlap the ends of the wire a little and stitch several times to secure.

2 Stitch the wings with 3799(2) and 3865(2) using long and short stitch. Add French knots with 3799(2).

3 Cut out with a ⅛ in. (3 mm) margin all around. Using fabric glue, secure the fabric to the back of the wings.

4 Attach the upper wings to the base fabric.

Sewing line

Cutting line

Butterfly motif and pincushion template at actual size

1 Mark a 4 x 4 in. (10 x 10 cm) square in the center of the green linen. Transfer (see page 106) the embroidery motif from the template (above), marking the antenna, body, and lower wings of the butterfly on the green linen, and the upper wings on the white lightweight cotton (A).

A

B

Embroider the body, lower wings, and antennae onto the green linen following the stitch instructions on page 16. Follow the instructions on page 18 to embroider the upper wings on the white cotton, and sew the wings to the base fabric along both sides of the butterfly body. Cut out the marked pincushion square (B).

C

3 Place the green linen and the off-white linen with the right sides together. Machine stitch around the edge of the fabric, leaving a 2⅜-in. (6-cm) opening for turning. Trim the corners and turn right side out (C).

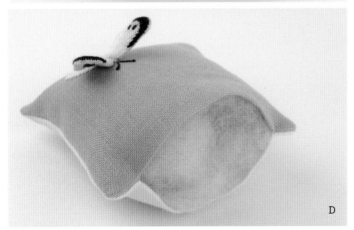

D

4 Press out any wrinkles and fill with your choice of stuffing material (D).

5 Sew the opening closed using ladder stitch (E). Shape the butterfly wings as desired.

E

Spring snowflake scissors case

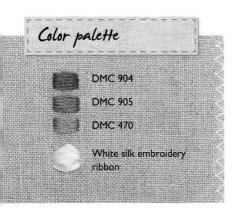

DMC 904

DMC 905

DMC 470

White silk embroidery ribbon

Appearing in late winter to early spring, these bell-shaped blossoms bring cheer to gardens, forests, and meadows, and can do the same in your sewing box. Embroidered with silk ribbon and edged with beads, this scissors case is elegant, yet practical. The suede lining keeps the scissors protected, while the snap closure ensures that they stay inside. From the delicate embroidery to the final edging stitch, the entire case is sewn by hand.

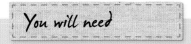

You will need

Fabric (L x W)
Exterior: Beige linen, 9 x 14 in. (23 x 35 cm)
Lining: Cotton muslin, 8 x 9½ in. (20 x 24 cm) *
Interior: Beige faux suede, 8 x 8 in. (20 x 20 cm)
Interfacing: Iron-on interfacing 8 x 8 in. (20 x 20 cm)

Thread
DMC #25 embroidery floss, color 904
DMC #25 embroidery floss, color 905
DMC #25 embroidery floss, color 470
Silk embroidery ribbon, white, ⅛ in. (3 mm) width

Other
Sewing thread to match the exterior fabric
Two-part snap closure
350 dark green seed beads, size 11/0

* The lining serves to hide the seams and add structural strength. Since it won't show much (just a line along the edge, if the bead trim does not cover it), you can use whatever you have on hand, but be sure to choose a color that won't show through the linen. A plain, lightweight cotton like muslin in a color to match your exterior fabric is a good choice.

Stitches for the motif
Flower: Ribbon stitch. Add a French knot at the bottom of each petal using 905(1).
Stem: 905(1) Stem stitch.
Leaf: 470(2), 905(2), 904(2) Gradation stem stitch filling, with the lightest color on the stem side.

Finished dimensions: Approximately 6 x 2¾ in. (15.5 x 7 cm), to fit a pair of scissors approximately 5⅛ in. (13 cm) long and 1¾ in. (4.5 cm) wide at the handles

Method

1 Cut a square of linen 9 x 9 in. (23 x 23 cm). Cut two interfacing pieces, following the pattern (right). Center one interfacing piece on the back of the linen and iron in place. Mark the cutting line on the front of the linen and transfer the embroidery motif (see page 106) from the template (right), making sure that the flowers are centered on the interfacing. Embroider following the stitch insturctions on page 20. This is the exterior front.

2 Cut all the fabric pieces following the pattern. There should be two each of the exterior (one is embroidered, the other is plain), lining, and suede. Attach the second interfacing piece to the exterior back linen. Mark the sewing line on the two lining pieces.

3 With right sides together, sew together the exterior front and one lining piece using running stitch, leaving a 2-in. (5-cm) opening on one side for turning. Clip the top curves and cut notches around the bottom curve (A). Trim the seam allowance to ³⁄₁₆ in. (5 mm) and turn right side out. Sew the opening closed using ladder stitch. Repeat for the exterior back.

The numbered petals show the order in which they should be stitched

2
1   3

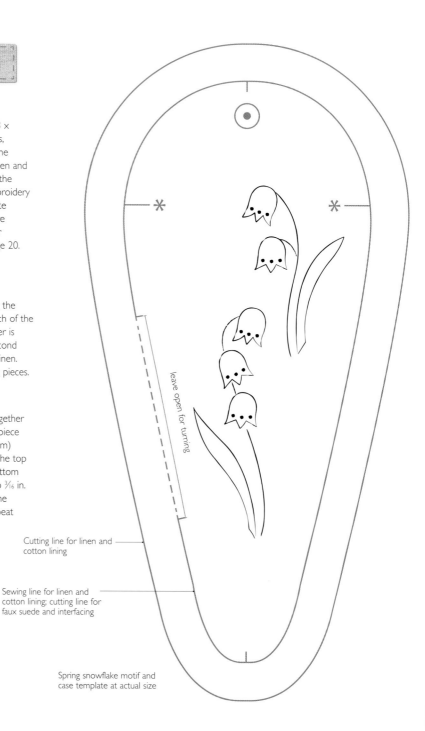

leave open for turning

Cutting line for linen and cotton lining

Sewing line for linen and cotton lining; cutting line for faux suede and interfacing

Spring snowflake motif and case template at actual size

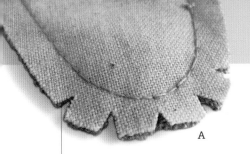

A

Cut notches in bottom curve
to make fabric sit evenly when
turned.

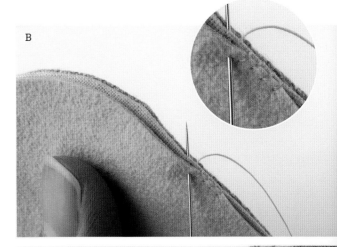

B

C

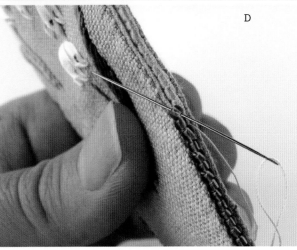

D

4 Sew one part of the snap closure onto
one piece of faux suede, as indicated on
the pattern, and the second part onto the
second piece of faux suede. Attach the suede
piece with the stud side of the snap closure to
the lining side of the exterior front using whip
stitch (B). Repeat with the second suede
piece—with the socket side of the snap
closure—and the exterior back.

5 With suede sides together, sew the
bottom portion of the front and back
together from * to *, as shown on the pattern
(C). Make small running stitches so that the
stitching is inconspicuous.

6 To sew seed beads along the edge on the
front lining layer, start on the right edge
where the top portion separates, and pick up
two beads on the needle. * Take a back stitch
the length of one bead and take the needle
through the second bead again (D). Pick up
two more beads and repeat from * until you've
gone all the way around.

7 After the last two beads have been
attached, take the needle through the very
first bead and pick up two more beads. Sew
these down along the back lining layer of the
top portion and continue as for the front until
the point where the layers meet. Take the
needle through the bead at the intersection
and secure the thread.

Daffodil hanger cover

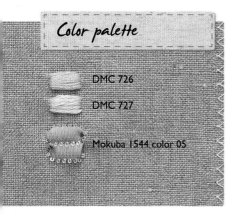

Color palette

DMC 726

DMC 727

Mokuba 1544 color 05

This special cover will give your plain wire hangers a fresh new look, with the flower peeking out between the collar of a jacket, or above the neckline of a dress. Make a collection in a variety of colors and trumpets—variegated ribbon is used here, but a solid color would result in flowers just as sweet. The daffodil template includes a few leaves, but here these have been left out, and a green gingham contrast added at the bottom of the hanger instead. The contrast fabric has been cut on the bias, but depending on the preferred look, it can be taken along the grain too.

You will need

Fabric (L × W)
Main: Off-white linen, 15¾ × 19¾ in. (40 × 50 cm)
Contrast: Green gingham, 14½ × 14½ in. (37 × 37 cm) if on bias, 4¾ × 19 in. (12 × 48 cm) if along grain

Thread
DMC #25 embroidery floss, color 727
DMC #25 embroidery floss, color 726

Other
Mokuba 1544 color 05
Pearl bead, ⅛ in. (3 mm)
DMC #25 embroidery floss, color 703 (if using)
Fray preventer

Stitches for the motif
Flower petals: 727(2) Outline with split stitch along the top half of the petal, then fill with long and short stitch. Switch to 726(2) closer to the center. Leave a space unstitched for sewing on the corona.

Flower (corona or "trumpet"): 2¾ in. (6 cm) of variegated ribbon, gathered into a circle. Sew a row of running stitch along the yellow side and pull on the thread so gathers form. Secure in a circle and stitch down in the center of the petals. Sew a pearl bead in the center.

Leaves: not shown on this project. 703(4) two-spoke woven picot stitch (see page 118). When you reach the top, hide the thread end by tucking it in the woven leaf on the back side, being careful not to distort the stitch.

TIP
To prevent fraying, use a tiny amount of fray preventer on the cut ribbon edges.

NOTE
Hanger sizes do vary, so make sure the hanger you want to cover will fit inside the template provided on page 124.

Finished dimensions: Approximately 16¼ in. (41.5 cm) wide at the base, 6 in. (15.5 cm) tall, to fit a hanger that is 16 in. (41 cm) wide at the base and 4¼ in. (11 cm) tall to the base of the neck

Method

Daffodil motif at
actual size

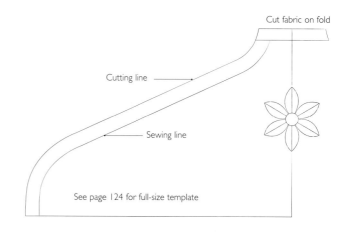

Cut fabric on fold

Cutting line

Sewing line

See page 124 for full-size template

A

B

C

1 Mark the pattern (see page 124) on the off-white linen. Transfer the embroidery motif (see page 106) from the template (above), and embroider following the stitch instructions on page 24. The leaves are not included here, but you can add them in if you prefer.

2 Cut all the fabrics according to the pattern (A). The gingham can be cut on the bias, as shown here, or horizontally along the grain.

3 Zigzag stitch along the neck seams on both the front and back fabrics. Fold down the seam allowance to the wrong side of the fabric and machine stitch in place (B).

4 Prepare the contrast fabric trim by folding half the width of the seam allowance on one long edge toward the wrong side. Fold the same amount again, encasing the raw edge, and machine stitch in place. Zigzag stitch along the other long edge (C).

5 With right sides together, sew the gingham and linen along the bottom edge on both the front and back fabrics. Make sure that the edge with the zigzag stitch on the gingham aligns with the linen. Press the seam allowance toward the gingham side.

6 Machine stitch the seam allowance in place from the right side (D).

7 With right sides together, sew the shoulder edges together (E).

8 Apply fray preventer along the shoulder seams. Turn right-side out.

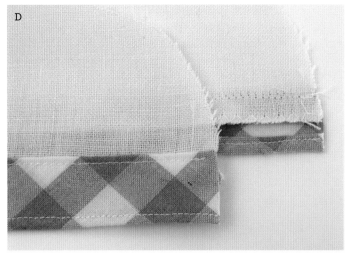

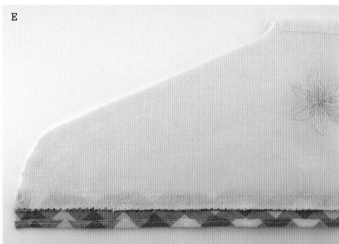

. . . .

TIP

If necessary, make a couple of slits along the shoulder curve to lessen the bulk (F). Be sure to finish the cut edges with a touch of fray preventer.

Red clover cushion cover

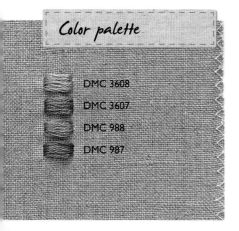

Color palette

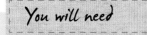

DMC 3608

DMC 3607

DMC 988

DMC 987

Adding a new cover to a sofa cushion can be a quick and easy way to redecorate. Embroidered on green gingham for a fresh, springtime look, this cover is simple to sew up with a few straight seams and an envelope-style opening. Resizing and rearranging the red clover motif—and many of the other motifs—can work for larger projects like this too. Place a few for a corner accent, as here, or scatter a handful across the entire surface for a little clover patch of your own. Make additional covers with motifs like the spring speedwell and dandelion, and you'll have a field of spring wildflowers right in your home.

You will need

Fabric (L × W)

Front: Green gingham, 14 × 14 in. (35 × 35 cm)

Back: Off-white linen, 12¾ × 9½ in. (32 × 24 cm), two pieces

Thread

DMC #25 embroidery floss, color 3608

DMC #25 embroidery floss, color 3607

DMC #25 embroidery floss, color 988

DMC #25 embroidery floss, color 987

Stitches for the motif

Flower: Holding 3607(1) and 3608(2) together, fill with lazy daisy stitch starting at the top.

Stems and sepals: 987(2) Stem stitch.

Leaves: 987(2), 988(2) Fishbone stitch, starting at the stem edge. Round out the form at the end.

Finished dimensions: Approximately 12 × 12 in. (30 × 30 cm), to fit a cushion of the same size

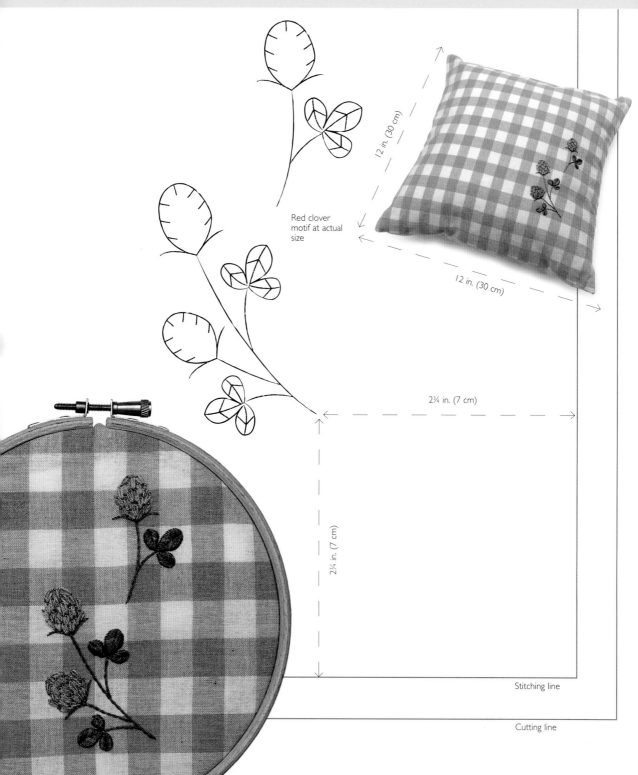

Red clover
motif at actual
size

12 in. (30 cm)

12 in. (30 cm)

2¾ in. (7 cm)

2¾ in. (7 cm)

Stitching line

Cutting line

Method

1 Mark a 12¾ x 12¾-in. (32 x 32-cm) square on the green gingham. Transfer the embroidery motif (see page 106) from the template (left), aligning the right corner of the square with the pattern (A). Embroider according to the motif directions. Cut the green gingham along the marked square.

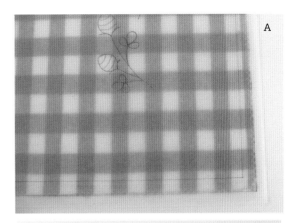

2 Zigzag stitch around the entire gingham and along the two short edges and one long edge of the linen pieces (B).

3 On the two back pieces, fold down ⅜ in. (1 cm) of the raw edge to the wrong side, then fold the same amount again to encase the edge. Machine stitch in place.

4 Place the embroidered gingham piece right-side up in front of you. Position the top piece of the back linen, wrong-side up, on top of the gingham with the zigzag-stitched edge aligned with the top edge of the gingham. Then place the bottom piece of the back fabric, wrong-side up, on top of that with the zigzag-stitched edge aligned with the bottom edge of the gingham. Make sure the finished seams are toward the middle. Pin in place (C).

5 Machine stitch all around the square, then turn right-side out (D).

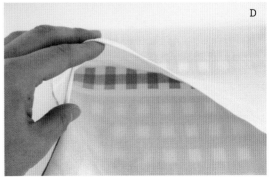

A year in stitches
Summer

Wild strawberry, see page 40

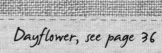

Dayflower, see page 36

Snail, see page 121

Sunflower, see page 121

Bee, see page 123

Cosmos, see page 44

Beetle, see page 121

Safflower, see page 121

Morning glory, see page 121

Fern, see page 52

Ranunculus, see page 48

Queen Anne's lace, see page 121

Dayflower drawstring bag

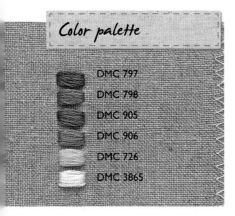

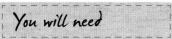

Color palette

DMC 797
DMC 798
DMC 905
DMC 906
DMC 726
DMC 3865

Drawstring bags are simple to make and infinitely useful. This version, featuring the dayflower motif, is made from a medium-weight cotton chambray with a blue-on-blue color scheme. Toss in a few essentials to take on the go or use it to keep small items from getting lost in a larger tote. This project can easily be adapted to other weights of fabric too. For example, a pale, lightweight cotton will result in a dainty, feminine pouch, while using a coarse, heavyweight linen will give a rustic, utilitarian alternative.

You will need

Fabric (L × W)
Blue medium-weight cotton chambray, 13⅜ × 18⅛ in. (34 × 46 cm)

Thread
DMC #25 embroidery floss, color 797
DMC #25 embroidery floss, color 798
DMC #25 embroidery floss, color 905
DMC #25 embroidery floss, color 906
DMC #25 embroidery floss, color 726
DMC #25 embroidery floss, color 3865

Other
⅜-in. (1-cm) wide herringbone tape, blue, 47¼ in. (120 cm)
Fray preventer

Stitches for the motif
Flower petals: 797(2), 798(2) Long and short stitch. Start with a row of 797 and work the rest in 798.
Pollen: 726(2) French knots.
Stamens: 3865(1) Stem stitch.
Flower base: 905(1) + 906(1) Satin stitch. Hold the two colors together.
Flower stem: 905(1) + 906(1) Stem stitch. Hold the two colors together.
Leaves: 905(2) Outline with split stitch. Fill with satin stitch from the leaf edge to the center vein.
NOTE: Because the leaves on the bottom flower are small, omit the split-stitch outline.

Finished dimensions: Approximately 9½ × 7½ in. (24 × 19 cm)

Method

Dayflower motif
at actual size

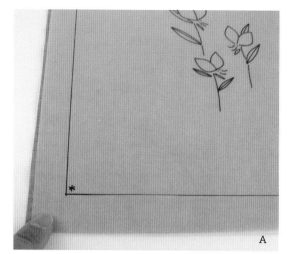

A

B

C

1 Mark a rectangle on a piece of tracing paper, 11 × 8¼ in. (28 × 21 cm). Place the dayflower motif 2⅛ in. (5.5 cm) from the bottom edge of the marked rectangle and center it width-wise. Transfer the embroidery motif (see page 106) (A).

2 Embroider the motif according to the stitch directions on page 36. Cut the fabrics to size. There should be two pieces measuring 11 in. (28 cm) long and 8¼ in. (21 cm) wide (B).

3 Using a sewing machine, zigzag stitch all around the edges (C).

D

E

4 With right sides together, machine stitch down one side, along the bottom, then up the other side, starting and stopping 2 in. (5 cm) from the top edge (D).

5 For the remaining 2 in. (5 cm) of the side seams, fold ⅜ in. (1 cm) of the edge toward the wrong side and stitch down, making sure to work the layers separately. Repeat for the remaining three edges (E).

6 To make the drawstring casing, fold ⅜ in. (1 cm) of the top edge down toward the wrong side, then fold down ¾ in. (2 cm) again to encase the zigzag-stitched edge. Machine stitch close to the bottom edge (F). Repeat for the other side. Turn the bag right-side out.

7 Cut two pieces of herringbone tape, each 23⅝ in. (60 cm) long. Treat the ends with fray preventer. Fold ¼ in. (7 mm) toward the wrong side and sew down each side (G).

8 Thread the first drawstring from right to left along the front casing, then back again from left to right along the back casing. Tie the ends together. Thread the second drawstring the opposite way, from left to right along the front casing, then back from right to left along the back casing (H). Tie the ends together.

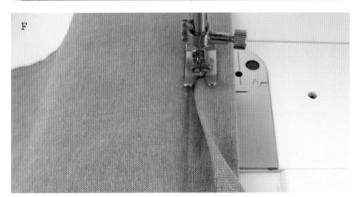

F

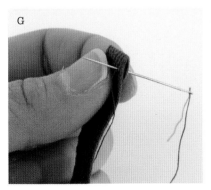

G

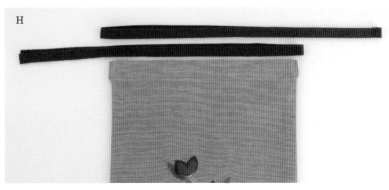

H

Strawberry key chain

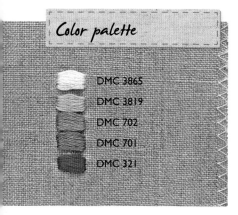

Color palette

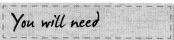

DMC 3865

DMC 3819

DMC 702

DMC 701

DMC 321

Stitch a mini version of the strawberry motif for a key chain that's dainty and sweet. Embroidered on a polka-dot fabric and sewn onto a felt base, this project is great for showing off both dimensional and flat embroidery. To create the plump berry, the strawberry is embroidered on a separate fabric first, then stitched in place. This key chain will make a pretty addition to your key ring, or an accent to your bag, if attached to the handle, strap, or zipper. It's also a good take-along project, since all the sewing is done by hand.

You will need

Fabric (L x W)

Main: Light green cotton with white polka dots, 4¾ x 4¾ in. (12 x 12 cm)

Felt: Green felt, 5½ x 2¾ in. (14 x 7 cm)

Stumpwork fabric: Red lightweight cotton 3⅛ x 3⅛ in. (8 x 8 cm)

Batting: Lightweight quilt batting 2¾ x 2¾ in. (7 x 7 cm)

Thread

DMC #25 embroidery floss, color 3865
DMC #25 embroidery floss, color 3819
DMC #25 embroidery floss, color 702
DMC #25 embroidery floss, color 701
DMC #25 embroidery floss, color 321

Other

Stuffing of your choice (optional)
Cardstock in desired thickness, 2¾ x 2¾ in. (7 x 7 cm)

Craft glue (for adhering felt)
Key chain of your choice

Stitches for the motif

Berry stem: 701(1) Stem stitch.

Flower petals: 3865(1) Outline with split stitch, 3865(2) fill with satin stitch.

Flower center: 3819(1) French knots.

Leaves: Top leaf with 702(2), bottom leaf with 701(2). Outline with split stitch, fill with satin stitch from the leaf edge to the center vein.

Strawberry (dimensional work): (see page 110).

Berry cap: 702(2) 2-spoke woven picot. Make the point of the picot just beyond the pattern line, create the woven picot, then stitch the loose thread down right on the pattern line.

NOTE: Stitch the cap before attaching the strawberry.

Finished dimensions: Medallion measures approximately 2¹⁄₁₆ in. (5.3 cm) in diameter

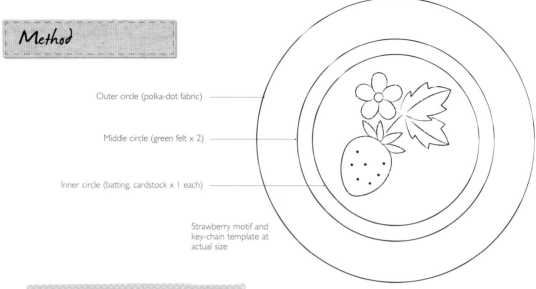

Method

Outer circle (polka-dot fabric) ——————

Middle circle (green felt × 2) ——————

Inner circle (batting, cardstock × 1 each) ——————

Strawberry motif and
key-chain template at
actual size

A

1 Mark the circle for the polka-dot fabric
(see pattern, above), and center the motif
within it. Transfer the embroidery motif
(see page 106) (A).

2 Embroider the motif according to the
stitch instructions on page 40. Be sure to
stitch the strawberry on the red cotton
first and attach to the polka-dot fabric using
the method on page 110 (B).

3 Cut the polka-dot fabric, felt, batting, and
cardstock as indicated by the pattern
(above) (C).

B

C

D

4 Glue the quilt batting to one side of the cardstock (D).

5 Sew around the embroidered fabric circle using running stitch, about ¼ in. (7 mm) from the edge (E). Do not knot the thread.

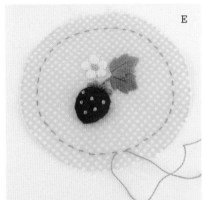

E

6 Center the cardstock/quilt batting on the wrong side of the fabric, so that the side with the quilt batting is facing the fabric. Gently pull the thread so that the fabric gathers toward the back over the cardstock. Adjust the gathers so that they are even all around (F). Secure the thread by sewing across the circle.

7 To attach the key chain, place the bottom ring of the chain on the wrong side of one of the pieces of green felt, so that the top third of the ring sticks out beyond the edge of the felt. Sew the bottom portion of the ring to the felt, about ¼ in. (6 mm) wide (G).

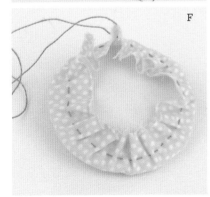

F

8 Center the embroidered circle on the felt circle with the key chain, making sure to arrange the motif so that the top of the design aligns with the key chain. Sew down using ladder stitch (H).

9 Place the second felt circle beneath the first felt circle. Sew the two layers of felt together along the edge of the embroidered medallion with running stitch (I).

G

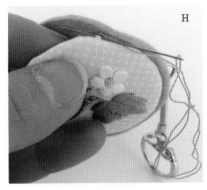

H

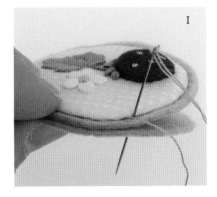

I

Cosmos compact mirror

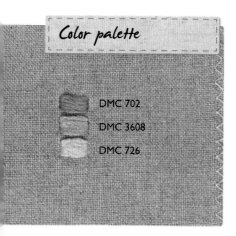

Color palette

DMC 702

DMC 3608

DMC 726

Touching up your makeup could become something to look forward to with a compact mirror like this one. This version is with the cosmos motif in a classic pink, but it would look just as lovely in red-violet, white, orange, bicolor, or even brown for the chocolate cosmos. Or choose a different flower—any round bloom would work just as well. If it doesn't quite fit, reduce the motif to size. Just keep in mind that surface embroidery works best if you are going to be tossing it in your bag.

You will need

Fabric (L x W)

Main: Off-white linen, 4¾ x 4¾ in. (12 x 12 cm)

Batting: Lightweight quilt batting, 3⅛ x 3⅛ in. (8 x 8 cm)

Thread

DMC #25 embroidery floss, color 702
DMC #25 embroidery floss, color 3608
DMC #25 embroidery floss, color 726

Other

Compact mirror with removable front disk
Paper
Craft glue (for adhering fabric and metal)

Stitches for the motif

Flower petals: 3608(1) Long and short stitch.

Flower center: 726(2) French knots.

Leaves: 702(1) Stem stitch.

Flower base (for side-facing flower): Not used in this project. 703(2) Straight stitches to fill.

Flower buds: Not used in this project. 917(2), 3608(2) Outline with split stitch, fill with padded satin stitch. Base of bud with 703(2) satin stitch on horizontal.

Flower stems: Not used in this project. 703(2) Stem stitch

Finished dimensions: size of compact, as chosen: the removable disk in this version measures 2¼ in. (5.7 cm) in diameter, and the pattern provided is for this size

Method

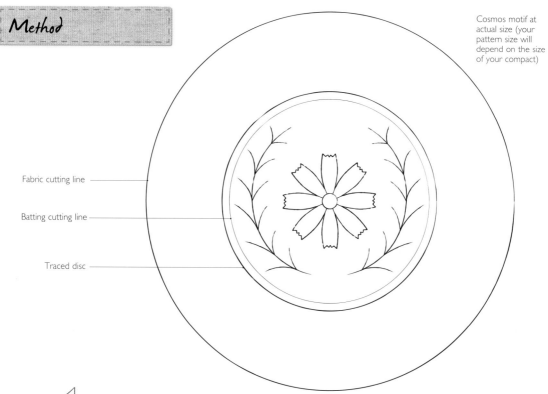

Fabric cutting line

Batting cutting line

Traced disc

Cosmos motif at actual size (your pattern size will depend on the size of your compact)

1 To make the pattern, remove the circular metal disk from the front of the compact (A). Place the disk on a piece of paper and trace around it (B). Add ¾ in. (2 cm) to the radius and draw another circle around the first. This is the pattern for the fabric.

2 Draw another circle just inside the circle of the metal plate, about ¹⁄₁₆ in. (2 mm) in. This is the pattern for the batting.

3 Cut out the paper pattern along the fabric line and mark the pattern on the linen fabric. Transfer the embroidery motif (see page 106) from the template (above), making sure it is centered in the circle. Embroider following the stitch instructions on page 44 (C).

4 Cut the pattern along the batting line and use this pattern to cut the batting.

A

B

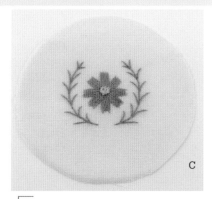

C

D

E

5 Glue the batting to the front of the compact's removed circular metal disk (D and E).

6 Cut the embroidered fabric along the pattern line, as marked in Step 3. Sew around the circle using running stitch, about ⅜ in. (1 cm) from the edge (F). Do not knot the thread.

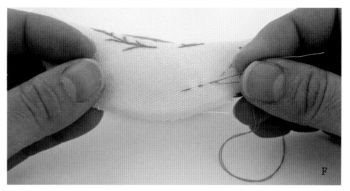

F

7 Center the embroidery on the batting. Turn it over and gently pull the thread so that the fabric gathers toward the back. Adjust the gathers so that they are even all around. Secure the thread by sewing across the circle (G).

G

8 Apply glue to the front of the compact, where you removed the disc from (H). Place the covered disc over it, press down, and hold until attached.

H

Ranunculus phone cover

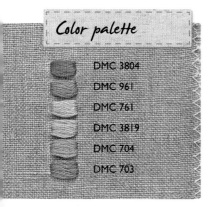

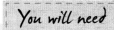

Color palette

DMC 3804

DMC 961

DMC 761

DMC 3819

DMC 704

DMC 703

Protect your phone from scratches with a pretty ranunculus cover. The version shown here is for an iPhone 6, but with the provided formula, you'll be able to make a custom cover for your phone. This design uses a ready-made plastic cover for securing the phone to the case and a magnetic button closure for easy opening and closing.

Ranunculus motif at actual size

You will need

Fabric (L × W)

As calculated by formulas (see fabric requirements, page 50)

Exterior: Green linen

Interior: Vine cotton print

Interfacing: Iron-on interfacing

Thread

DMC #25 embroidery floss, color 3804

DMC #25 embroidery floss, color 961

DMC #25 embroidery floss, color 761

DMC #25 embroidery floss, color 3819

DMC #25 embroidery floss, color 704

DMC #25 embroidery floss, color 703

Other

Plastic cover to fit smartphone of choice (non-transparent)

Magnetic button, 9/16 in. (1.4 cm) diameter

Fine-grade sandpaper (240 grit)

Extra-strength craft glue (for adhering fabric and plastic)

Stitches for the motif

Flowers: 761(3), 961(3), 3804(3) Couched circles, sewn down at random with one strand of floss to match.

Flower center: 3819(3) Three French knots.

Flower bud: 961(2) Outline in split stitch, fill with padded satin stitch (two layers). Sepals in 704(2) straight stitch.

Flower stems: 704(3) Wrapped stem stitch.

Leaves: 703(2) Stem in stem stitch, leaves in lazy daisy stitch.

Finished dimensions: To fit a smartphone of your choice

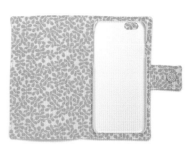

The inside of the finished case with the plastic holder in place

The magnetic button closure is secure, but still easy to open

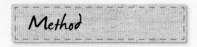

Method

Fabric requirements

Measure the length and width of your plastic smartphone cover. Set y as the length, x as the width, and z as the thickness. So it's not too tight to cover, add $\frac{1}{16}$–$\frac{1}{8}$ in. (2–3 mm) to the thickness for z.

Length: $y + 1\frac{5}{16}$ in. (y + 3.4 cm)

Width: $2x + z + 1\frac{7}{8}$ in. (2x + z + 4.8 cm)

This formula will give you the exact fabric size you need for the cover portion, including seam allowance for both exterior and interior fabrics. You will need one piece of each. Remember to add extra to the exterior fabric as necessary in order to fit the fabric in the embroidery hoop or frame. You'll need to mark out the actual fabric size on the exterior fabric before attaching the interfacing.

For the cover interfacing, subtract ¾ in. (2 cm) from the length and width measurements as determined by the above formula. You will need two pieces.

The closure band measures z + 2¼ in. long and 2 in. wide (z + 5.5 cm long and 5 cm wide), including seam allowance. Cut one piece each of the exterior and interior fabrics. Subtract ¾ in. (2 cm) from both length and width for the interfacing size. Cut two pieces of interfacing.

The plastic case shown here is for an iPhone 6 and measures 5⅜ in. (13.7 cm) long, 2¾ in. (7 cm) wide, and ¼ in. (7 mm) thick.

A

1   Determine the amount of fabric and interfacing you need using the formula (left). On a piece of paper, draw out the fabric, interfacing, and phone case lines as shown in the diagram (below), and place the ranunculus motif in the phone case rectangle as desired. This is your pattern. Mark the rectangle for the fabric size on the green linen.

2   Attach interfacing to the exterior and interior fabrics, centered on the wrong side. Transfer the embroidery motif (see page 106) onto the left half of the linen (A). Embroider following the stitch instructions on page 48. If you added extra fabric all around for framing, then cut the fabric to pattern size.

3   With the right side facing up, mark the location of the magnetic button on the linen. Lay the washer so that the center lies 1 1/16 in. (2.7 cm) from the right fabric edge and centered lengthwise. Draw the slits through the washer and cut (B).

4   Take the socket side of the button and push the prongs through (C). Turn the fabric over, place the washer over the prongs, and bend the prongs flat.

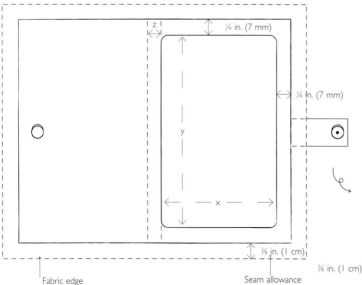

z

¼ in. (7 mm)

¼ in. (7 mm)

y

x

⅜ in. (1 cm)

⅜ in. (1 cm)

Fabric edge

Seam allowance

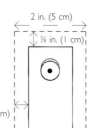

2 in. (5 cm)

⅜ in. (1 cm)

5 To prepare the closure band, attach interfacing to the exterior and interior fabrics, centered on the wrong side (D). Mark the button location on the right side of the interior fabric so that the center of the button measures $^{15}/_{16}$ in. (2.3 cm) from the short end. Attach the stud side of the button in the same way as the socket side (E).

6 With right sides together, machine stitch the exterior and interior fabrics for the band together, leaving the end away from the button open. Trim the top corners and turn right-side out.

7 Layer the fabrics with right sides together. Tuck the closure band in place as determined by the pattern. The button should be facing toward the interior fabric, and the raw fabric edge should align with the fabric edges (F).

8 Machine stitch all around, leaving an opening of 3½ in. (9 cm) for turning on the side with the button attached to the cover (socket side). Trim all corners and turn right-side out. Sew the opening closed using ladder stitch (G).

9 Lay the cover with the interior facing up. Take the plastic case and lightly go over the side to be glued down with sandpaper for better adhesion. Center the plastic case on the right half of the cover and glue in place, following the directions on the craft glue packaging. Be sure to apply just enough so that the glue doesn't seep out from the fabric (H).

B

C

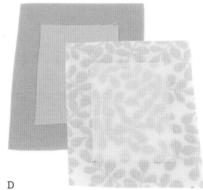

D

E

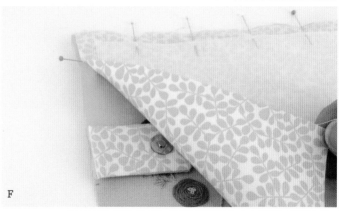

F

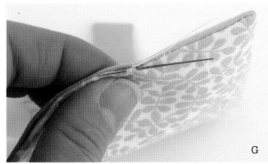

G

H

Fern leaf shirt

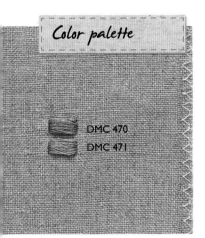

Color palette

DMC 470
DMC 471

With the addition of a little embroidery, a ready-made shirt can be easily transformed into a one-of-a-kind piece. This version features the fern leaf motif on the back of a denim shirt, for a fresh and sporty look. Placed on the yoke just below the collar, it's subtle and stylish. And since there's no sewing up involved, it's a quick and easy project for those who simply want to embroider.

Fern motif at actual size

Align with shirt center

You will need

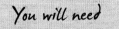

Light blue denim shirt

Thread
DMC #25 embroidery floss, color 470
DMC #25 embroidery floss, color 471

Stitches for the motif
Leaves: 470(2) Outline with split stitch, fill with padded satin stitch (one layer).
Stem of leaves: 471(2) Split stitch.

Finished dimensions: Size of shirt, as chosen

Method

1 Lay the shirt in front of you with the back facing up. For this shirt, the center back is where the yoke dips down to form a point. For other shirts, this may be where there is a hang loop or a box pleat. If there is no center detail, fold the yoke in half and make a crease to mark the center. Center the fern motif on the yoke.

2 Transfer the embroidery motif (see page 106), and embroider according to the motif directions (left).

Bittersweet, see pages 58 and 122

Cattail, see page 121

Dragonflies, see page 121

Rudbeckia, see page 62

A year in stitches
Fall

Japanese maple, see page 74

Acorns, see page 70

Chestnut, see page 122

Gingko, see page 74

Japanese bellflower, see page 122

Aster, see page 66

Chinese tallow, see page 122

Billy button, see page 122

Bittersweet oven mitt

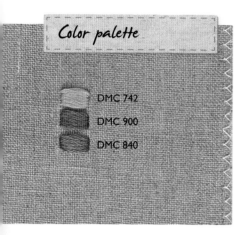
Fall signals the start of the busy baking season, and the bittersweet oven mitt will see you through it all. An attractive vine with vibrant orange berries and dark yellow shells, the embroidered bittersweet will add a bright spot to any kitchen. The horizontal arrangement works well in a panel, so it is applied here as a band along the cuff. Since it's not stitched directly on the hand, it won't see as much wear; and once the hand does wear out, you can remove the band and attach it to another and it will be as good as new.

You will need

Fabric (L × W)

Exterior linen band: Beige linen, 6¾ × 5½ in. (17 × 14 cm)

Exterior main: Gingham linen, 19½ × 10¼ in. (50 × 26 cm)

Exterior contrast band: Burnt orange cotton, 6¾ × 6 in. (17 × 15 cm)

Interior: Quilted cotton 19½ × 13 in. (50 × 33 cm)

Hanging loop: Burnt orange cotton, 4 × 1⅝ in. (10 × 4 cm)

Thread

DMC #25 embroidery floss, color 742
DMC #25 embroidery floss, color 900
DMC #25 embroidery floss, color 840

Stitches for the motif

Branch: 840(3) Stem stitch for the main branch, 840(2) stem stitch for the side branches.

Berries: 900(2) Padded satin stitch (over an asterisk shape).

Shells: 742(2) Fly stitch.

Finished dimensions: Approximately 6 in. (15 cm) wide at wrist, 11 in. (28 cm) long

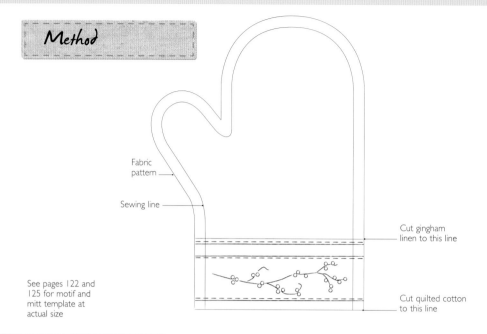

Method

Fabric
pattern

Sewing line

Cut gingham
linen to this line

Cut quilted cotton
to this line

See pages 122 and
125 for motif and
mitt template at
actual size

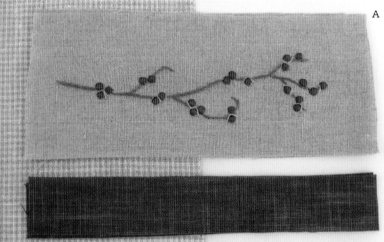

A

B

C

1 Mark the exterior linen band following the pattern (see page 126) on the beige linen. Transfer the embroidery motif (see page 106) from the template on page 122 and embroider according to the directions. Cut the embroidered band along the marked rectangle.

2 Cut all fabrics following the patterns. There should be two each of all the pieces, except for the hanging loop (A). Cut just one additional linen band as the other linen band is the embroidered piece made in step 1.

3 To make the hanging loop, fold 3/16 in. (5 mm) of each of the long edges toward the wrong side of the fabric (B), then fold in half. Sew the long edge closed and machine stitch along the other long edge. Fold in half to form a loop (C) and sew in place.

4 Assemble the exterior hand in the following order: machine stitch contrast band A to the main fabric along the bottom edge with right sides together. Press seam to

the main fabric side. Then machine stitch the linen band to contrast band A with right sides together. Press the seam to the linen side. Next, machine stitch contrast band B to linen band with right sides together (D). Press seam to the linen side. Following that, machine stitch all seam allowances in place from the right side.

5 Repeat the above process for the exterior hand back, replacing the embroidered linen band with a plain linen band.

6 Layer the fabrics in the following way: one interior-fabric (quilted cotton) piece with right-side facing down, both exterior fabrics with right sides together, and the second interior fabric with right side facing up. The exterior fabrics should extend past the interior fabrics at the wrist. Tuck the hanging loop between the exterior fabrics as indicated. The edges of the loop should align with the edge of the fabrics. Pin everything in place (E).

7 Machine stitch along the hand portion of the mitt, from one corner of the wrist to the other. Do not sew along the wrist edge. Trim the seam allowance to about ¼ in. (7 mm). Clip the seam allowance between the thumb and the hand.

8 To prevent the edge from fraying, zigzag stitch all around the hand portion, starting and ending with the edges of the quilted fabric (F). Turn right-side out.

9 Fold the bottom edge of the exterior fabric up to meet that of the interior. Fold up again along where the two fabrics meet so that the raw edges are encased. Sew in place using ladder stitch (G).

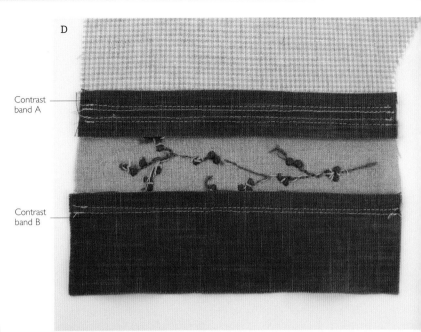

D

Contrast band A

Contrast band B

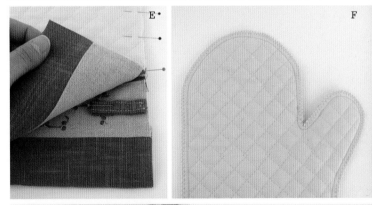

E

F

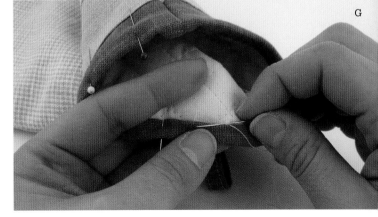

G

Rudbeckia apron

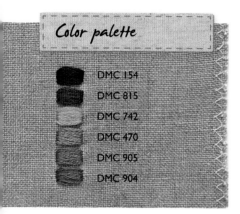

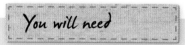

Color palette

DMC 154

DMC 815

DMC 742

DMC 470

DMC 905

DMC 904

Make an impact in and out of the kitchen with a bright, bold rudbeckia bloom embroidered on your apron pocket. Paired with a subtle, moss green striped fabric, the colorful flower gives the apron a warm, autumnal look. The original motif has been enlarged quite a bit, which works for the stitches used in this design. Not all motifs can take a size alteration without changing the stitches, so be sure to make a test sample if you are choosing a different motif. Since aprons require frequent washing, it's best to choose flat, surface embroidery.

You will need

Fabric (L × W)

Apron: Moss green striped cotton, 20½ × 29⅛ in. (52 × 74 cm) for body; 8 × 8 in. (20 × 20 cm) for pocket

Lining for pocket: Muslin or lightweight cotton in a light color, 8 × 8 in. (20 × 20 cm)

Thread

DMC #25 embroidery floss, color 154
DMC #25 embroidery floss, color 815
DMC #25 embroidery floss, color 742
DMC #25 embroidery floss, color 470
DMC #25 embroidery floss, color 905
DMC #25 embroidery floss, color 904

Other

Cotton herringbone tape, moss green, 1 in. (2.5 cm) width, 94¹⁄₁₆ in. (239 cm)
Fray preventer

Stitches for the motif

Flower petals: 742(2) Outline with split stitch along the top half of the petal, fill with long and short stitch. Switch to 815(2) closer to the center, as shown.

Flower center: 154(2) Padded satin stitch (two layers). For the front-facing flower, make one row of French knots around it; for the side-facing flower, make two rows of French knots along the base.

Leaf: 904(2), 905(2) Outline with split stitch, fill with satin stitch to the center vein. Half the leaf is filled with one color and half with the other, as shown.

Stem: 470(4) Whipped stem stitch.

Finished dimensions: Apron body measures approximately 27⁹⁄₁₆ in. (70 cm) wide and 18⅞ in. (48 cm) long; ties measure 29½ in. (75 cm) from edge of apron body

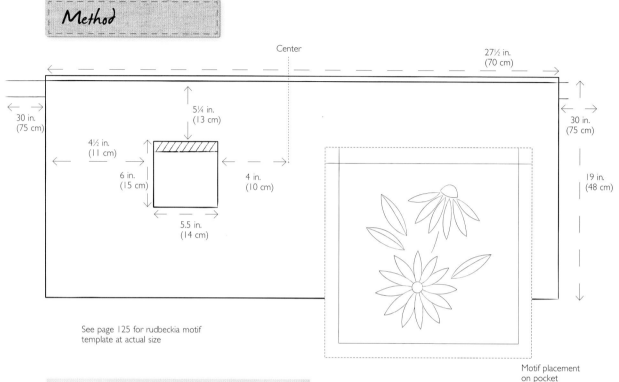

Method

Center

27½ in.
(70 cm)

5¼ in.
(13 cm)

30 in.
(75 cm)

30 in.
(75 cm)

4½ in.
(11 cm)

6 in.
(15 cm)

4 in.
(10 cm)

19 in.
(48 cm)

5.5 in.
(14 cm)

See page 125 for rudbeckia motif
template at actual size

Motif placement
on pocket

A

1 On tracing paper, draw a square 6¼ x
6¼ in. (16 x 16 cm). Draw a horizontal
line ½ in. (1.25 cm) below the top line.
Draw a horizontal line ⅜ in. (1 cm) above the
bottom line and inside the two sides of the
square. Center the embroidery motif inside
the resulting square. Transfer the embroidery
motif onto the striped cotton pocket fabric
(see page 106) (A).

B

2 Place the striped pocket fabric on top of
the pocket lining fabric, with the wrong
sides together. Machine stitch the two
fabrics together just inside the marked pocket
square (dotted line) to secure the layers (B).
Embroider through both layers of fabric
following the stitch instructions on page 62.
Cut out the 6¼ x 6¼-in. (16 x 16-cm) square.

3 To finish the top edge of the pocket, cut a piece of herringbone tape 6¼ in. (16 cm) long. Fold in half and place over the top edge of the pocket. Machine stitch in place (C). Fold a ⅜-in. (1-cm) seam allowance on the remaining three sides toward the back and press in place.

4 To prepare the apron body, fold ⅜ in. (1 cm) of the fabric on the two short sides toward the wrong side of the fabric, then fold the same amount again to encase the raw edge. Machine stitch in place (D).

5 Along the top and bottom edges of the apron, fold ⅜ in. (1 cm) toward the wrong side, then fold the same amount again to encase the raw edge. Machine stitch in place (E).

6 Align the pocket on the apron body as shown in the pattern (left), and machine stitch in place. Sew over the beginning and the end a few times to better secure the pocket (F).

7 To prepare the waistband/tie, cut a length of herringbone tape 88 in. (224 cm). Treat both ends with fray preventer, then fold ⅝ in. (1.5 cm) to the wrong side and sew down.

8 Lay the herringbone tape on the apron body so that the top edge of the tape lies along the top line of stitching and is centered widthwise (G). Starting on one side of the apron body, machine stitch along the top edge of the tape across the body of the apron. When you reach the other end, sew down along the side, back across the bottom of the tape, then up along the other side (G close-up).

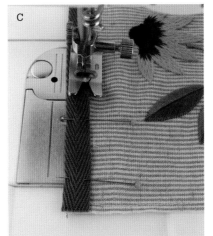

C

D

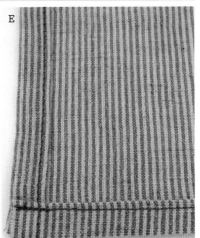

E

F

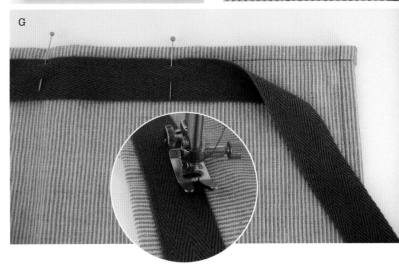

G

Aster napkin ring

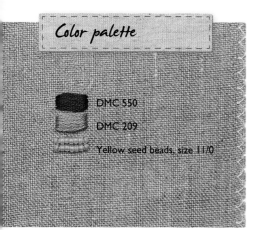

Color palette

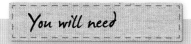

DMC 550

DMC 209

Yellow seed beads, size 11/0

Asters are cheerful little fall flowers that are great for creating color variations. Purple, magenta, pink, red, white, or yellow; you can choose a color to match the rest of your table linens, or make one in each for a coordinating set of napkin rings. Since these asters are one of the easier motifs to embroider and the napkin rings equally easy to sew up, this project is a good option for beginners. Embroidery on wool tweed gives the napkin ring a warm and inviting look, while the rhinestones add a touch of sparkle, dressing up your table for a truly special meal.

You will need

Fabric (L x W)

Embroidered band: Off-white wool tweed, 9 x 4 in. (23 x 10 cm)

Iron-on interfacing: 6¾ x 1⅝ in. (17 x 4 cm)

Base band: Purple cotton, 7½ x 2⅞ in. (19 x 7.3 cm), two pieces

Thread

DMC #25 embroidery floss, color 550

DMC #25 embroidery floss, color 209

Other

Approximately 20 yellow seed beads, size 11/0

Two sew-on rhinestones with silver base, ⅛ in. (3 mm)

Stitches for the motif

Large flowers: 550(3) Lazy daisy stitch. Fill the center randomly with seed beads.

Small flowers: 209(2) Granitos stitch, three passes. Sew the rhinestone in the center.

Finished dimensions: Approximately 7 in. (18 cm) around, 2 in. (5 cm) wide

A

1 Mark the rectangle for the embroidered band according to the pattern (right) on the woolen fabric. Center the interfacing on the back and press to attach.

2 Transfer the embroidery motif (see page 106) to the front of the woolen band. Embroider following the stitch instructions on page 66. Cut out the embroidered band to 7½ x 1¾ in. (19 x 4 cm), making sure the embroidery is centered both vertically and horizontally (A).

B

3 Fold the seam allowance on the long edges of the embroidered band toward the wrong side. Center this piece on one of the base fabric pieces so that about ⅝ in. (1.5 cm) of it shows on either side of the embroidered band. Machine stitch in place (B).

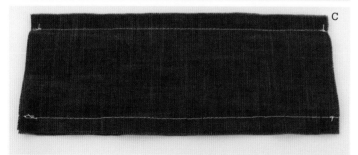

C

4 Lay the embroidered band right-side up in front of you. Place the second base band fabric on top of it, so that the right sides are together. Machine stitch along the two long sides, leaving both short sides open (C). Turn right-side out.

5 Tuck the seam allowance on the short ends into the opening. Sew the ends closed using ladder stitch (D).

D

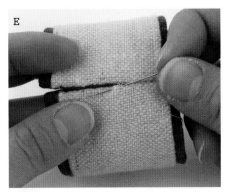

6 Sew the short ends together using ladder stitch to form a ring (E). For a secure join, sew the seam with the right side facing out first, then flip it inside out and sew the seam again from the interior side (F).

Aster motif and band template at actual size

Sewing line

Cutting line

Acorn egg cozy

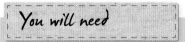

Color palette

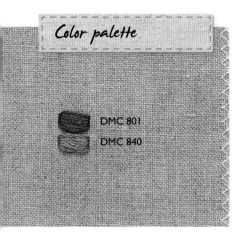

DMC 801

DMC 840

Eggs will take center stage on your table with this charming acorn egg cozy. Since it's as much decorative as it is useful, an egg cozy is a great canvas for trying out dimensional techniques like the acorn motif, which has been reoriented here to better suit the design space. Make it a pair with the chestnut motif (see page 122) for a fun, nutty set. Or try other dimensional motifs from different seasons—the butterfly would be lovely for spring occasions, such as an Easter brunch or on Mother's Day.

You will need

Fabric (L x W)
Exterior: Beige linen, 4½ x 9½ in. (11 x 24 cm)
Interior: Brown cotton, 5 x 9½ in. (12 x 24 cm)

Thread
DMC #25 embroidery floss, color 801
DMC #25 embroidery floss, color 840

Other
Brown felt to match DMC 801, 2 x 2 in. (5 x 5 cm)

Stitches for the motif
Acorn: 801(2) Padded satin stitch (with felt, one layer).
Cap: 840(6) Fill with rows of coral stitch.
Branch: 840(3) Stem stitch.
Stem: 840(3) Straight stitch.

Finished dimensions (measured flat):
Approximately 3 in. (7.5 cm) tall,
3¼ in. (8 cm) wide

Method

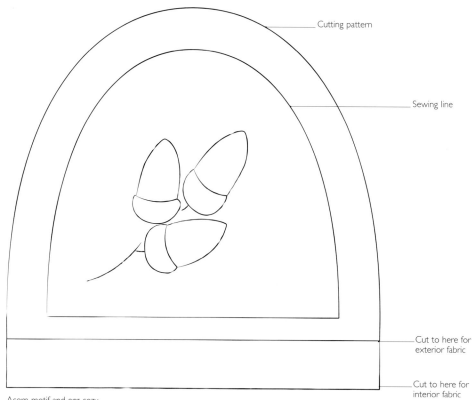

Cutting pattern

Sewing line

Cut to here for exterior fabric

Cut to here for interior fabric

Acorn motif and egg cozy
template at actual size

Finished egg cozy complete
with acorn motif

1 Mark the egg cozy pattern (left) on the exterior fabric. Transfer the embroidery motif (see page 106) from the template (left) and embroider following the stitch instructions on page 70.

2 Cut the exterior and interior fabrics as indicated on the pattern. There should be two pieces of each (A).

3 Place the exterior pieces with right sides together. Machine stitch together along the curved edge. Trim the seams to 3/16 in. (5 mm) and clip the curves. Press the seams open. Repeat for the interior (B).

4 Turn the exterior piece right-side out. Tuck the interior piece into the exterior. The interior should extend out from the exterior edge by about 1/2 in. (1.2 cm).

5 Fold the bottom edge of the interior fabric up to meet that of the exterior. Fold up again along where the two fabrics meet so that the raw edges are encased, and pin (C).

6 Sew in place using ladder stitch (D).

A

B

C

D

Fall leaves coaster set

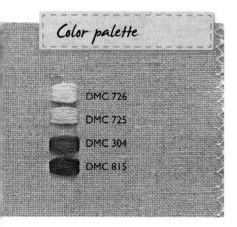

Bring fall colors to the table with this fall leaves coaster set. Inspired by pressed leaves tucked between thick, fabric-covered books, the stitched leaves look much like the perfectly preserved ones from many seasons past. The embroidery on the olive green fabric has a scholarly feel that would look great not just in the dining room but in the home office as well. When selecting other motifs, be sure to go with surface embroidery as there will be a mug sitting on top of it. For coasters with a crisp finish, use interfacing as instructed here, but if you prefer your coasters soft, just skip that step.

You will need

Fabric (L x W)

Front: Green cotton, 12 x 7 in. (30 x 18 cm)

Interfacing: Iron-on interfacing, 4 x 4 in. (10 x 10 cm), 2 pieces

Back: Gingham linen, 4¾ x 4¾ in. (12 x 12 cm), 2 pieces

Thread

DMC #25 embroidery floss, color 726

DMC #25 embroidery floss, color 725

DMC #25 embroidery floss, color 304

DMC #25 embroidery floss, color 815

Stitches for the motif

Japanese maple

Leaves: 304(2), 815(2) Outline with split stitch, fill with satin stitch from the leaf edge to the center vein. Each lobe of the leaf is stitched half with one color and half with the other. On the top leaf, the right half of each lobe is filled with 815; on the bottom leaf, the right half of each lobe is filled with 304, and the left half with 815.

Stems: 815(2) Stem stitch.

Ginkgo

Leaves: 725(2), 726(2) Outline with split stitch along the top edge. Fill with long and short stitch, the first row with 725, the rest with 726.

Stems: 726(2) Stem stitch.

Finished dimensions: Approximately 4 x 4 in. (10 x 10 cm)

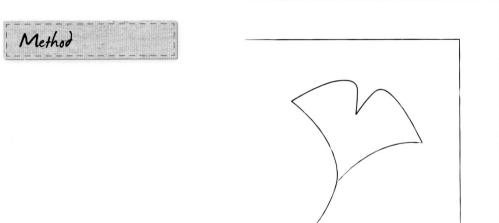

Method

Japanese maple, ginkgo motifs and coaster templates at actual size

This diagram shows the placement of the ginkgo leaf on the coaster

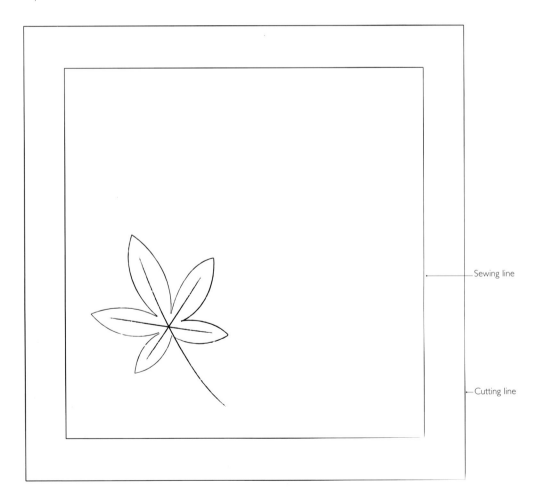

Sewing line

Cutting line

A

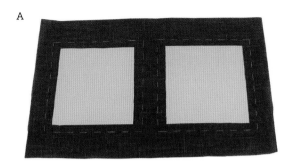

1 Mark two coaster squares on the green cotton according to the pattern (left). Baste two 4¾ x 4¾-in. (12 x 12-cm) squares on the green cotton. Center the interfacing on the back of the marked squares and press to attach (A).

2 Transfer the Japanese maple motif (see page 106) from the template (left) to one green square and the gingko motif (left) to the other. Embroider following the stitch instructions on page 74 (B). Cut out the coaster squares along the basted stitches.

3 With right sides together, machine stitch around the edge of the fabric, leaving an opening for turning. Trim the corners (C) and turn right-side out (D).

4 Use ladder stitch to sew the opening closed (E). Press out any wrinkles.

B

C

D

E

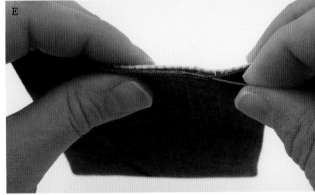

Yew sprig, see page 86

Flowering kale, see page 90

A year in stitches
Winter

Hellebore, see page 122

Snowflakes, see page 123

Witch hazel, see page 123

Cyclamen, see page 123

Plum branch, see pages 98 and 123

Ivy, see page 123

Snowberries, see page 82

Pine bough, see page 122

Camellia, see page 94

Snowberry brooch

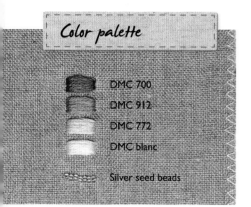

Color palette

DMC 700

DMC 912

DMC 772

DMC blanc

Silver seed beads

Stitch a single snowberry motif for a brooch to adorn your dress, jacket, or scarf. A cluster of stumpwork berries topped with silver beads, the snowberries make a striking contrast against the black felt for an elegant, sophisticated look. By changing the color of the background felt, you can easily change the impression of the brooch to suit your style. Whether for a formal occasion or a fun night out, the snowberry brooch will add just the right finishing touch to your outfit.

You will need

Fabric (L × W)
Black felt, 6⁵⁄₁₆ × 5⅛ in. (16 × 13 cm)

Thread
DMC #25 embroidery floss, color 700
DMC #25 embroidery floss, color 912
DMC #25 embroidery floss, color 772
DMC #25 embroidery floss, color blanc

Other
Six ³⁄₁₆-in. (5-mm) round wooden beads
Seven ¼-in. (6-mm) round wooden beads
13 silver seed beads, size 11/0 (2 mm)
Brooch pin, 1-in. (2.5-cm) long
Craft glue (for adhering felt)

Stitches for the motif
Berries: Blanc(1), 772(1) Stumpwork berries with a seed bead on top (see page 111). Make seven with blanc using ¼-in. (6-mm) round wooden beads and three each with blanc and 772 using ³⁄₁₆-in. (5-mm) round wooden beads.
Stem: 912(2) Stem stitch.
Leaves: 700(2) Outline in split stitch, fill with satin stitch from the leaf edge to the center vein.

Finished dimensions: Approximately 2⅞ in. (7.3 cm) tall and 1⅛ in. (2.8 cm) wide

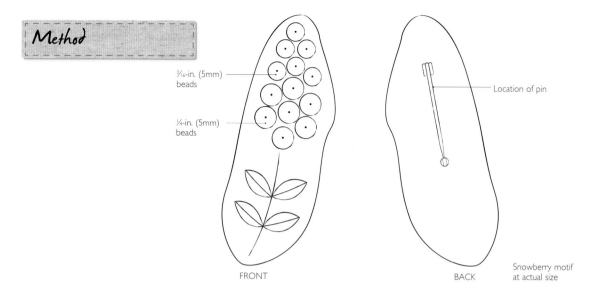

Method

3/16-in. (5mm) beads

1/4-in. (5mm) beads

FRONT

Location of pin

BACK

Snowberry motif at actual size

1 Transfer the embroidery motif (see page 106) onto one half of the piece of felt (A). The stumpwork berries should be marked with just a center dot.

2 Make the snowberries (see page 111). Embroider the stem and leaves following the stitch instructions on page 82, then attach the berries (B and C).

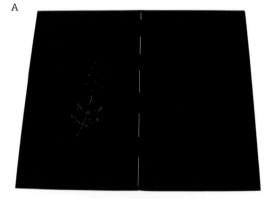

A

B

C

3 Cut the embroidered motif out with a margin of about ⅜ in. (1 cm) (D). Layer the cut piece on top of the remaining piece of felt and cut another piece of about the same shape.

4 Sew the brooch pin vertically onto the plain piece of felt. The pin should be placed behind where the stumpwork berries will be, as shown (E).

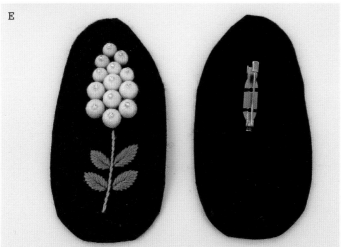

5 Glue the two pieces of felt together with the wrong sides together. Let dry.

6 Trim the felt down (F) to the margin shown in the pattern (left).

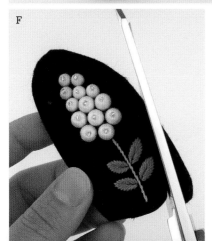

Barrette with yew sprig

Color palette

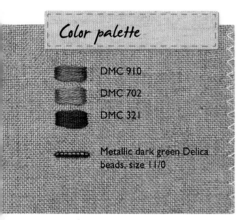

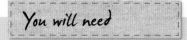

DMC 910

DMC 702

DMC 321

Metallic dark green Delica beads, size 11/0

A barrette is a great platform for showing off dimensional embroidery like the yew branch. This motif uses the stumpwork technique of wrapping a wooden bead with embroidery thread and topping it with a bead for lifelike berries. An example of how portions of motifs can be applied, this design uses a single branch of yew to fit in the narrow space of the barrette. To make the berries really stand out, the embroidery is padded with batting to create a little lift, and framed by black felt to add contrast. The resulting barrette is a fun and festive way to accessorize for the holiday season.

You will need

Fabric (L x W)
Front fabric: Linen, 6¼ x 5⅛ in. (16 x 13 cm)
Backing fabric: Black felt, 4 x 1³⁄₁₆ in. (10 x 3 cm)
Interfacing: Iron-on interfacing, 3⁹⁄₁₆ x ¾ in. (9 x 2 cm)
Batting: Lightweight quilt batting, 3¹¹⁄₁₆ x 1¹¹⁄₁₆ in. (9.3 x 4.3 cm)

Thread
DMC #25 embroidery floss, color 910
DMC #25 embroidery floss, color 702
DMC #25 embroidery floss, color 321

Other
Eight ¼-in. (6-mm) round wooden beads
Eight metallic dark green Delica beads
Cardstock, 3⁹⁄₁₆ x ¾ in. (9 x 2 cm)
Craft glue (for adhering fabric and metal)
Barrette clasp, 3⅛ x ⅜ in. (8 x 1 cm)

Stitches for the motif
Berries: 321(1) Make eight stumpwork berries with Delica bead on top (see page 111).
Stem: 702(2) Stem stitch.
Leaves: 910(2) Granitos stitch, four passes.

Finished dimensions: Approximately 4 in. (10 cm) long and 1³⁄₁₆ in. (3 cm) wide

Method

Linen size

Felt size

Cardstock and interfacing size

Batting size

Yew sprig motif and barrette
template at actual size

A

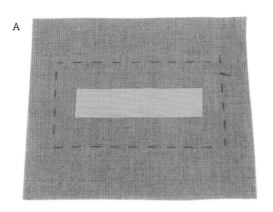

1 Baste a rectangle measuring 4¾ × 2⅜ in. (12 × 6 cm) in the center of the linen. Center and attach the iron-on interfacing to the wrong side of the linen (A).

2 Align the embroidery template according to the pattern (above) and transfer the embroidery motif (see page 106). The leaves should be marked with a line and the berries marked with just a center dot (B).

B

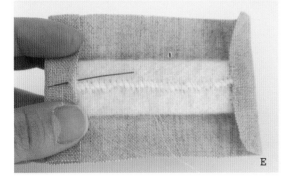

3 Make the yew berries (see page 111). Embroider the stem and leaves following the stitch instructions on page 86, then attach the berries (C). Cut the fabric along the basted stitches.

4 Place the batting with the wrong side facing up and center the cardstock on top of it. Bring the long edges together to the center of the cardstock and whip stitch together (D).

5 Place the embroidered linen with the wrong side facing up and center the batting/cardstock piece on top of it. Fold the short ends in and sew down (E).

6 Fold ³⁄₁₆ in. (5 mm) of the long edges to the wrong side, then fold again so that the edges meet in the center (F). Sew together using ladder stitch. Sew both ends closed.

7 Center the embroidered piece on top of the black felt. Sew all around using ladder stitch to attach (G).

8 Apply craft glue to the back of the barrette clasp. Center the clasp on the back of the embroidered piece and attach. Sew down the clasp on the short ends through the holes (H).

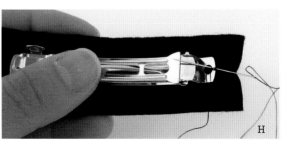

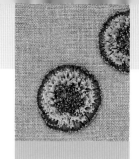

Flowering-kale necklace

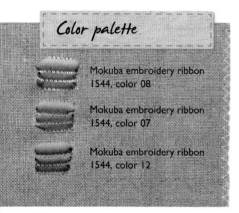

This cute, playful necklace features two shades of flowering kale. To create the frilly leaves, color gradation ribbon is gathered and sewn down in a circle. Depending on your choice of chain and arrangement of the kale rosettes, the impression of the necklace can change completely, so experiment with different combinations to reflect your own personal taste. Here, three in a cluster on a delicate chain results in a colorful, bohemian look. In the garden, the attractive leaves of the flowering kale offer a pretty show all through the colder months.

You will need

Fabric (L × W)
Off-white felt, 8 × 8 in.
(20 × 20 cm)

Thread
Mokuba embroidery ribbon 1544,
color 08
Mokuba embroidery ribbon 1544,
color 07
Mokuba embroidery ribbon 1544,
color 12
Sewing threads to match the color of
the ribbons

Other
Fray preventer, optional
Necklace chain with clasp, 15¾ in.
(40 cm)
Three round jump rings, size
1/16 × 3/16 in. (1 × 5 mm)

Three oval jump rings, in a size that suits
your necklace chain
Craft glue (for adhering felt)
Pliers

Stitches for the motif
Gathered ribbon flower (see pages
92–93) in spiral rounds.

Finished dimensions: Necklace chain
measures 15¾ in. (40 cm); kale rosette
measures approximately 1⅜ in. (3.5 cm)
in diameter

TIP
To prevent the ribbon from fraying, use a tiny amount of fray preventer on the cut edges of the ribbon.

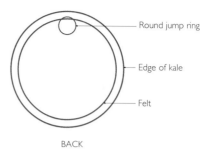

- Round jump ring
- Edge of kale
- Felt

BACK

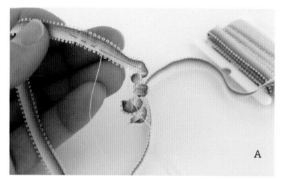

A

B

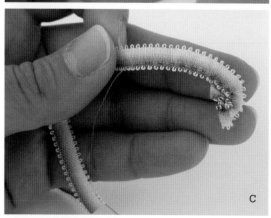

C

Light kale: Ribbons 08 and 12

1 Start with color 08. With the ribbon still attached to the spool, sew a row of running stitch along the lighter edge of the ribbon, pulling on the thread from time to time to create gathers as you go (A).

2 Once you have a length of gathered ribbon, thread another needle with sewing thread to match and sew down the gathered ribbon in a spiral onto the base felt fabric, starting in the center (B). If you don't have enough ribbon gathered, just sew more running stitch and gather as you go.

3 When you have almost reached the end of two rounds, cut the ribbon and secure the thread used for gathering. Finish the round by sewing down the end of the ribbon. Now sew a row of running stitch along the darker edge of the ribbon on the spool and create gathers as before (C). Continue to sew in a spiral around the sewn-down ribbon. When you have created two rounds, finish the ribbon as before.

4 Switch to color 12. Sew a row of running stitch along the light green side of the ribbon and create gathers as before. Continue to sew in a spiral around the previously sewn-down ribbon. When you have created one round, finish the ribbon as before.

Dark kale: Ribbons 07 and 12
as above.

Start by sewing along the lighter edge of color 07 ribbon, then on the darker edge. End with a round of color 12, sewing along the light green edge of the ribbon.

1 Cut the felt into four 4 x 4-in. (10 x 10-cm) squares. Mark a circle for each kale rosette on three of the squares of felt. Embroider following the instructions on page 92. Make two kale rosettes with 07 and 12, one with 08 and 12 (D).

2 Cut out the rosettes with a rough margin, so that the felt is slightly larger than the edge of the kale (E). From the remaining square of the felt, cut three circles about the size of the back of the rosette. Glue onto the back of the rosettes. Let dry.

3 Trim the felt so that it is about ¼ in. (7 mm) smaller all around than the edge of the kale. The felt should not show from the front.

4 Sew a round jump ring onto the felt at the top of each rosette below the ribbon edge, covering the bottom half of the ring (F).

5 Lay the necklace chain in front of you with the clasp side to the right. Determine the center of the necklace chain. Open an oval jump ring: hold the pliers in one hand and the jump ring in the other, and gently twist the ring open by pulling one side of the opening toward you and the other away from you. Do not pull open, or the ring will become distorted. Keep the opening as small as possible and slip onto the necklace chain. Measure 1⅜ in. (3.5 cm), or your preferred distance from the center, on either side and attach the remaining two oval jump rings. Attach rosettes to the jump rings with the embroidery side facing down and close the jump ring (G).

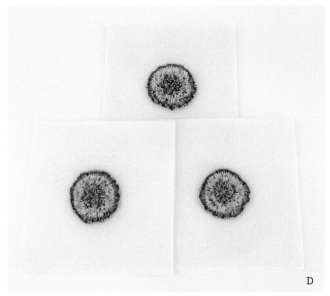

D

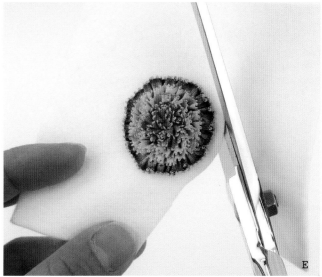

E

F

G

Camellia scarf

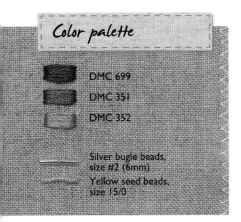

Color palette

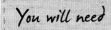

DMC 699

DMC 351

DMC 352

Silver bugle beads,
size #2 (6mm)

Yellow seed beads,
size 15/0

Adding some pretty embroidery can breathe new life into a familiar old scarf. This wool scarf has been given a subtle feminine look by attaching a single camellia blossom framed by a pair of leaves. The dimensional petals and leaves are outlined with wire and embroidered on separate pieces of fabric, then sewn onto the scarf. Whether the embroidery is flat or dimensional, creating the motifs on a separate fabric and sewing it on is a good method to use for fabrics that are tricky to embroider.

You will need

Wool scarf

Fabric
Lightweight cotton, peach
Lightweight cotton, green

Thread
DMC #25 embroidery floss, color 699
DMC #25 embroidery floss, color 351
DMC #25 embroidery floss, color 352

Other
Size #30 floral wire, white
Size #30 floral wire, green
Sewing thread, off-white
Silver bugle beads, size #2 (6mm)
Yellow seed beads, size 15/0
Craft glue (for adhering fabric)

Finished dimensions: Size of scarf, as chosen

Camellia motif at actual size

Method

A

Camellia petals:

1 Make two sets of petals. Couch down the white wire in petal form with 352(1), bending the wire as you go. When you reach the beginning, overlap the ends of the wire a little and stitch several times to secure.

2 Stitch the petals with 352(2) and 351(2) using long and short stitch, starting with 352 and switching to 351 closer to the center.

3 Using sewing thread, add standing beads to the center of the top set of petals by threading one bugle bead, then one seed bead (A). Take the thread back down the bugle bead and to the back of the fabric, skipping the seed bead (see page 111). Repeat to fill the center circle.

B

C

4 Cut out with a ⅛-in. (3-mm) margin all around. Clip straight in between the petals, close but not all the way to the wire (B). Be careful not to cut any embroidery threads. Also clip the curve at the top of the petals (C).

5 Using fabric glue, secure the fabric to the back of the petals (D).

Leaves (wired piece)

Make using the wire technique as used for the flower petals, with green floral wire and 699(2) satin stitch from the leaf edge to the center vein (E).

D

E

1 Embroider the camellia petals and leaves according to the motif directions. The flower should be embroidered on the peach fabric and the leaves on the green fabric. Bend the petals and leaves so that they form a slight arch.

2 Position the bottom set of petals (without center beads) so that the tip of the petal pointing straight down is 2⅜ in. (6 cm) from the edge of the scarf and centered widthwise (F).

3 Use small stitches, because they will show on the back, to sew down around the center circle (G). Place the top set of petals on the bottom set so that each petal sits between two petals below. Sew in place as before.

4 Tuck the ends of the leaves under the petals on either side of the flower and sew down both ends (H).

F

G

H

Plum-branch pouch

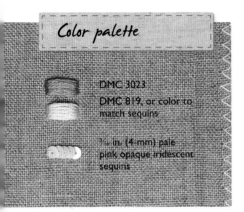

Color palette

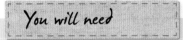

DMC 3023
DMC 819, or color to
match sequins

³⁄₁₆-in. (4-mm) pale
pink opaque iridescent
sequins

Embroidered on satin-back shantung with iridescent sequin blossoms, this sleek, zippered pouch works equally well as a mini clutch or a purse for small articles within a larger bag. To make the pouch suitable for being carried on its own, the lightweight shantung fabric is strengthened with interfacing to better hold its shape. To achieve a softer, more flexible pouch, skip the interfacing. Substituting the fabric with cotton or linen will result in a more casual, everyday pouch. For this version, the motif has been rotated to create a downward-reaching branch.

You will need

Fabric (L x W)

Exterior: Charcoal satin-back shantung, one piece measuring 10⅝ x 7 in. (27 x 18 cm)* and one piece measuring 9 x 5½ in. (23 x 14 cm)

Interior: Light beige satin-back shantung, two pieces measuring 9 x 5½ in. (23 x 14 cm)

Interfacing: Iron-on interfacing, four pieces measuring 9 x 5½ in. (23 x 14 cm)

* Add more fabric to this piece as necessary to fit in your embroidery hoop or frame.

Thread

DMC #25 embroidery floss, color 3023
DMC #25 embroidery floss, color 819

Other

Zipper, 7⅞ in. (20 cm)
³⁄₁₆-in. (4-mm) pale pink opaque iridescent sequins

Stitches for the motif

Flowers: Sew down five sequins in a circle. The sequins should be evenly spaced and slightly overlapped, with each stitch going from the center of the sequin to the center of the flower.

Buds: 819(2) Satin stitch.

Thick branch: 3023(2) Outline with split stitch, fill with satin stitch.

Thin branch: 3023(2) Stem stitch.

Finished dimensions: Approximately 8¼ x 4¾ in. (21 x 12 cm)

Method

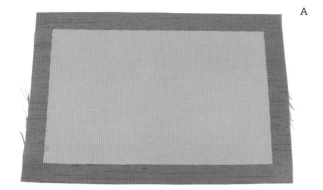

A

1. On the larger piece of exterior fabric, baste a rectangle measuring 9¹⁄₁₆ × 5½ in. (23 × 14 cm). If you are using interfacing, attach one piece in the marked rectangle on the non-satin side (A). Also attach one piece to the non-satin side of the other exterior fabric and one each to the satin side of the two interior fabrics.

2. Transfer the embroidery motif (see pages 106 and 123), and embroider following the stitch instructions on page 98. The sequin flowers should be marked with just a center dot. Cut out the pouch rectangle along the basted stitches (B).

B

3. To prepare the zipper, fold the extra length beyond the ends of the zipper toward the wrong side, as shown, and sew down (C).

4. Place the embroidered fabric right-side up in front of you. Align the zipper face-down along the top edge of the fabric (D). The zipper should be centered along this edge. For a right-handed version, the zipper pull should be to the left side; for a left-handed version, it should be to the right.

C

5. Place the interior fabric right-side down on top of the zipper. Baste the layers together by hand (E).

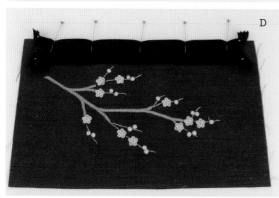

D

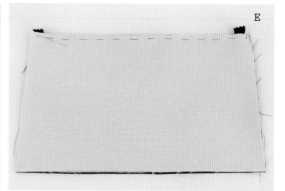

E

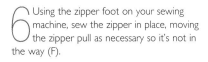

F

6 Using the zipper foot on your sewing machine, sew the zipper in place, moving the zipper pull as necessary so it's not in the way (F).

7 Flip the fabrics so that the zipper is exposed and the wrong sides of the fabrics are together. Machine stitch along the fabric edge by the zipper (G). Repeat steps 3–6 on the other side of the zipper with the remaining pieces of the exterior and the interior fabrics.

G

8 With the zipper pulled halfway open, flip the fabrics so that the right sides of the exterior fabrics and the right sides of interior fabrics are together (H). Make sure that the zipper teeth are facing toward the interior fabric. Sew around the edge, leaving an opening of 4¾ in. (12 cm) on the bottom of the interior fabric for turning.

9 Clip the bottom corners and turn right-side out (I).

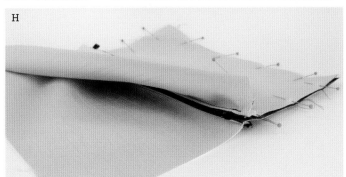

H

10 Sew the opening closed using ladder stitch (J). Tuck the lining inside the pouch.

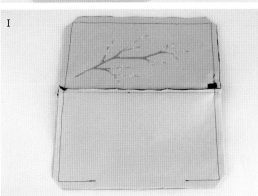

I

J

Tools

Needles (1)

Needles come in a variety of lengths and thicknesses with different eyes and points, so select the type that suits the thickness of thread chosen and the embroidery technique to be worked. Sizes with higher numbers indicate finer needles.

The following needles are used to create the embroidery in this book:

Crewel (embroidery) needles for embroidery with thread. Medium length with a long eye and a sharp point.
A: no.6 for 3–4 strands of floss
B: no.8 for 1–2 strands of floss
C: no.10 for 1 strand of floss
D: Chenille needle no.24 for ribbon embroidery. Longer in length and thick, with a large eye and a sharp point. The eye should be large enough to accommodate the width of the ribbon.
E: Cross stitch needle no.24 for making stumpwork berries, and for needleweaving.
Medium length with a blunt tip.
F: Beading needle no.10 for beadwork. Long and very fine with a narrow eye.
G: Sharps no.7 or 8 for hand sewing. Medium length with a small eye and a sharp point.

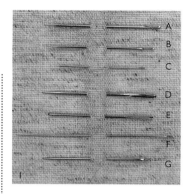

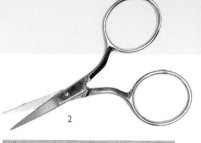

Scissors (2)

Embroidery scissors are ideal for snipping thread ends and for small trimming tasks. Those with a sharp point right to the tip are best. Have a designated pair for metallic threads as they can blunt the cutting edge.

Chain-nose pliers (3)

For bending floral wire to create wired dimensional pieces. The tapered jaws are flat on the inside and rounded on the outside.

Tracing paper (4)

For transferring embroidery designs onto fabric. Trace the selected design and place over dressmaker's carbon.

Tracer pen

A pointed pen without ink for tracing over an embroidery design placed over dressmaker's carbon.

Dressmaker's carbon (5)

Just like ordinary carbon paper, but for fabric. Choose the type that can be removed with water, unless you are certain that all markings will be covered.

Fray preventer (6)

A clear, liquid sealant that prevents cut edges of fabric from fraying. Apply to the ends of embroidery ribbon to keep them from unraveling.

Craft glue (7)

Glue for adhering various craft materials. There are products that can glue a wide range of things and others that are just for specific materials. Choose the type that suits the items that you will be gluing.

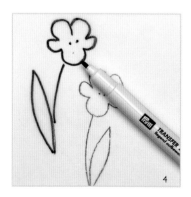

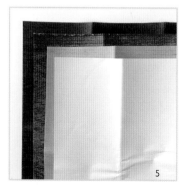

Hoops (8) and frames (9)

Keeping the fabric taut in an embroidery frame will allow for even stitching and reduce puckering and distortion of the fabric during the stitching process.

HOOPS

Hoops come in a variety of sizes, given by their diameter. Whenever possible, choose one that can hold the entire design so the hoop does not need to be shifted to complete the stitching. The inner ring may be wrapped with bias strips to protect the fabric and reduce slipping.

Adjust the screw of the outer ring so that it fits loosely over the inner ring. Place the fabric over the inner ring. Press the outer ring down over the fabric and the inner ring, making sure the fabric is taut. The area to be worked needs to be in the center of the ring. Tighten the screw to secure the fabric.

FRAMES

Interlocking bars are available in a variety of lengths so you can make a square or rectangular frame to fit any size embroidery. To create your frame, choose two pairs and simply slot the pieces together. Place the fabric over the frame with the right side up. Stretch the fabric evenly over the frame and pin in place using thumbtacks. Start at the center of the bar and pin out toward each side, keeping the pins close together. If desired, mount it on an embroidery stand or use a C-clamp and attach it to the edge of a table to free both hands for stitching.

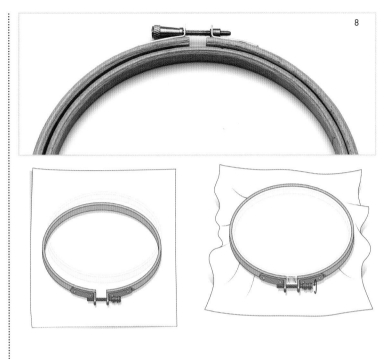

8

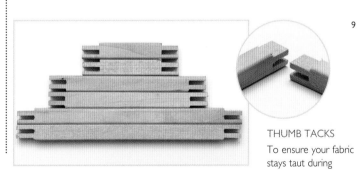

9

THUMB TACKS

To ensure your fabric stays taut during embroidery, you can use thumb tacks pushed into the wooden frame.

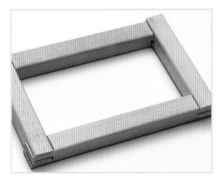

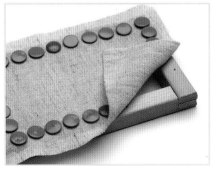

Materials

Fabric

Almost any fabric can be suitable for embroidery, but those with crispness and body are easier to handle. The fabric should be firm enough to support the stitching, with a weave that allows the thread or ribbon to pass through easily. The fabric can be plain or patterned, but should strike a good balance of texture and color with the embroidery design.

LINEN (1)

Linen is a plain-weave fabric that is available in a variety of weights. It is an ideal fabric for many types of embroidery and is easy to stitch on. Linen does wrinkle easily, but pressing with an iron while the fabric is still damp will remove most creases. Be sure to wash it first to pre-shrink it.

COTTON (2)

Cotton fabric is another good option for embroidery and is available in an array of weights and weaves. It's best to wash it once before embroidering. Plain, lightweight cotton fabric is suitable for making wired stumpwork pieces.

WOOL (3)

Depending on the type of wool fiber and the way it is woven, wool fabric can range from smooth and firm to coarse and loose. The ones with a looser weave can be harder to embroider and be prone to puckering when stitched. Attaching interfacing to the back can stabilize the weave and make it easier to handle.

Embroidery threads

There are many different types of threads available for embroidery, and they come in a variety of materials and thicknesses. Each has its own characteristics and produces different effects.

#25 COTTON EMBROIDERY FLOSS (4)

Most common of all the embroidery threads, #25 floss comes in a wide range of colors and can be used for most types of embroidery. It consists of six fine strands that can be divided as required. Hold multiple strands together to achieve the desired thickness.

METALLIC THREAD

Used to enhance embroidery with glittery effects. It comes on a spool or as a skein, and depending on the type, is divisible or non-divisible. Metallic threads are delicate and can be difficult to handle, so it's best to work with shorter lengths.

EMBROIDERY RIBBON (5)

Ribbon for embroidery comes in a variety of widths and materials. Silk embroidery ribbon is soft and pliable with a lovely sheen, and is versatile and easy to use. Variegated ribbon creates unique effects on its own without having to use multiple colors of ribbon.

Beads

Bugle beads are cylindrical tubes with a smooth or twisted surface. They come in a variety of lengths.
Seed, rocaille, or pony beads (6) are round but not perfectly spherical. They come in a range of sizes; the larger the number, the smaller the bead. The ones used in this book are 8/0, 11/0, and 15/0.
Delica beads are cylindrical seed beads that are very uniform in shape.
Wooden beads (7) Round wooden beads are used for making stumpwork berries. The hole of the bead can be small and rough on the inside, so use a pointed tool like the tip of a tracer or a sewing stiletto to enlarge the hole and smooth down the inside.

Sequins (8)

Decorative disks with a hole punched, usually in the center. Round sequins that are flat or cupped are most common, but they come in other shapes as well. Sizes for round sequins are given by their diameter in millimeters.

Rhinestones

Small glass crystals with multiple cut facets that catch the light for sparkle. They come in a variety of shapes and sizes and add a dramatic touch to a design. Sew-on types used with embroidery may have holes directly on the crystal or be attached to a setting with sew-on channels on the back.

Floral wire (wire stem, 9)

Thin, pre-cut pieces of wire used to create dimensional embroidery. Floral wire is commonly available in white and green, so choose the color that better suits the thread to be used. It comes in different gauges; the higher the number, the finer the wire. The size used in this book is #30.

Felt (10)

For padding embroidery to create dimension. Use a color that is close to the color of the thread that will be used to cover it. When using multiple layers, cut the top layer to the size of the pattern and each subsequent layer below a little smaller.

Filling (11)

Another option for padding dimensional embroidery. Filling is available in both natural and synthetic materials.

Fusible webbing

Heat-sensitive synthetic fiber backed with paper. When placed between two fabrics and heated with an iron, the fibers melt to fuse the fabrics together. It is used for appliqué.

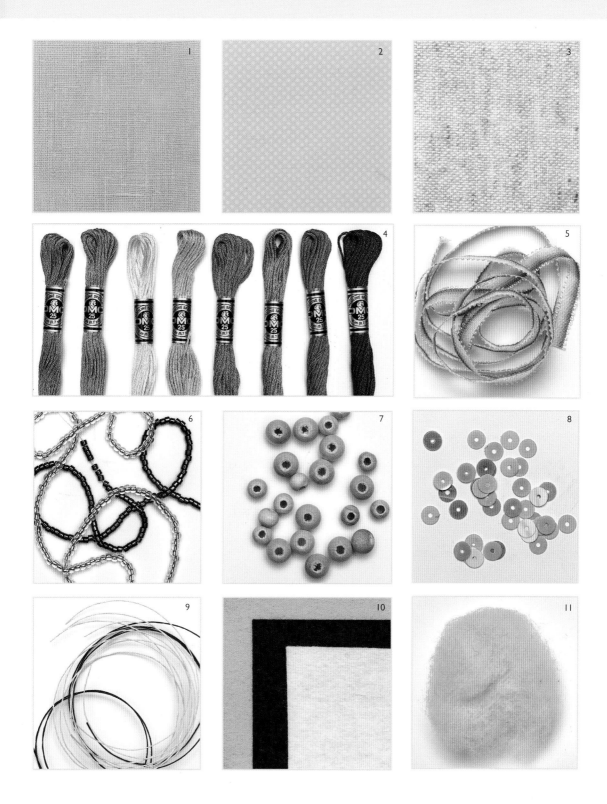

Getting started

Preparing fabric

Before embroidering, make sure to pre-shrink the fabric by washing it. Linen and cotton fabrics should be thoroughly soaked—at least an hour for linen, cotton can be less—then lightly spun and allowed to air dry. Do not wring, as this will cause wrinkles. When it is about halfway dry, press with an iron set to the appropriate setting to straighten the grain and dry it completely. If the fabric is pulling at the selvage edges and causing the fabric to pucker, make small cuts perpendicular to the selvage to release the tension.

Wool fabric should not be soaked, but misted with a spray bottle so it is damp. Let the moisture settle, then press with an iron set to the appropriate setting. Stop when there is still a hint of moisture left, then leave to air dry completely.

Transferring designs

There are several different ways of transferring a design onto fabric. Of these, two basic tracing methods are explained below. New products available today give the embroiderer other options, but whichever you choose, make sure the outline can be erased easily or completely covered with stitching.

USING A LIGHT BOX

Direct tracing of the design onto the fabric with the use of a light box is probably the simplest method of transfer for transparent materials. Electric or battery-operated light boxes are available in various sizes.

Place the design on the box, right-side up. Place the fabric over it so the design is lit from beneath and shows through the fabric. Trace the design using a transfer marker or, for dark fabric, white chalk.

USING DRESSMAKER'S CARBON

Dressmaker's carbon works in the same way as ordinary carbon paper. It comes in a variety of colors.

Place the fabric on a flat surface, right-side up. Place the design traced onto tracing paper on top of the fabric. Tuck a sheet of dressmaker's carbon between the fabric and the tracing paper with the carbon side toward the fabric. Carefully trace over the design using a tracer pen or a pen without ink.

Design decisions

Unless you decide to make a project exactly as it is given in the book, there will be a number of factors you'll need to consider in order to set up a design on a project.

SELECTING AND REARRANGING MOTIFS

As you begin to place motifs onto projects, you'll need to make certain decisions about the designs you choose. First, you'll need to select a motif that is suitable for the item and its end use. For example, it's not a good idea to choose stumpwork designs for things that require frequent laundering. Or when choosing where to embroider, avoid areas that are used frequently, like the hand of the oven mitt.

Once you have decided on the project and the motif, you'll need to consider the size and shape of the design space. In some cases, you may find that the motif needs to be altered to fit or look better visually. This can be done in a number of ways:

- Enlarging or reducing: Use a photocopier and specify the percentage you need.
- Flipping: Use a photocopier or trace onto tracing paper and flip the paper over.
- Rotating: Choose a stationary point on the motif and rotate using that as the center axis.
- Taking or moving parts: Use just a portion of the motif or move parts of the motif around. Copying the motif and cutting it up makes this easy to do.

- Combining: Choose elements from two or more motifs and combine them in a single design.

The asters on the napkin ring (right) is an instance in which three of the aster blooms were taken and placed in a row to fit on the narrow band. With the acorn egg cozy, the motif was flipped for a mirror image and rotated so that the acorns faced up rather than down. This way, the triangle formed by the three acorns mimicked the form of the egg cozy, which is wider at the bottom and narrower at the top.

To find the best arrangement for your project, draw the motif on a piece of tracing paper and place it in different positions so you can get an idea of what these would look like before you commit to a design. The tracing paper makes it easy to see the fabric beneath.

I

2

The original motif for the aster is a cluster of blooms (1). In order to suit the narrow napkin band, the original design had to be reworked (2).

HOW RESIZING CAN AFFECT THREAD REQUIREMENTS AND STITCH CHOICE

When you enlarge or reduce a design, it is sometimes necessary to make changes to accommodate the size change. One way to do this is by changing the number of thread strands used, as with the cosmos motif (right). The petals of the cosmos in the motif directory were stitched using two strands of thread, but this was changed to one strand on the reduced motif on the compact in order to maintain a similar level of fineness.

But not every stitch works with changes in thread count—some just become bulky instead of larger, others don't become as large as you need, and others still simply don't work at the desired size. In these instances, different stitches or methods may need to be chosen. For example, satin stitch doesn't work well on a large scale as the thread cannot span too far. To fill an enlarged motif, better options would be long and short stitch or appliqué. Just be

aware that while this may solve the issue of size, it may result in embroidery that doesn't have the same look or feel as the original.

Whatever changes you decide to make, it is always important to stitch up a sample before starting the actual project.

I

2

The cosmos design used on the directory page was completed using two strands of thread (1). For the compact project, only one strand of thread was used in order to keep the fineness of the design (2). The motifs are shown here at actual size for comparison purposes.

Working with threads

The motifs in this book use two types of thread: stranded cotton embroidery floss and metallic thread. Stranded floss is a versatile thread that consists of six fine strands loosely wound into a skein. Metallic threads can come stranded or single, in a skein or a spool.

DIVIDING STRANDED FLOSS

Cut a length of floss about 17–19-in. (43–48-cm) long. Threads that are too long can get worn while stitching and/ or lead to unwanted knots. Hold one end of the stranded floss in your left hand and separate the strands with your right hand. Pull the threads out one by one and combine the strands to achieve the required thickness. Make sure that the threads are not twisted together for better coverage and smoother stitching.

STARTING AND ENDING THREADS

Start your thread by making a knot at the end of the thread. Take the needle down through the fabric from the front and make three tiny backstitches in a spot that will be hidden with the embroidery. Work the first few stitches and cut off the knot. While a single knot to start the thread is not the preferred method, it can be used as necessary.

To end threads, take the needle through to the wrong side and run it in along the back of the stitches two or three times before trimming off the excess thread.

METALLIC THREAD

Metallic threads are delicate and liable to damage if they are not handled with care. To avoid this, work with shorter lengths, about 14–16 in (35–40 cm). If you have pulled out the stitches to re-stitch a couple of times, it's best to end that thread and switch to a new one. Stranded metallic thread can be divided in the same way as stranded cotton. Threads on spools can just be cut at the desired length.

Working with ribbon

Embroidery ribbon is used to create effects that are quite different from that of threads. Work with short lengths, as the ribbon may split and fray if it is passed through the background fabric too many times.

SECURING THE RIBBON TO THE NEEDLE (1)

Cut a length of ribbon about 12–13 in. (30–35 cm) long with the edge on a diagonal. Pass the ribbon through the eye of the needle. Because ribbon tends to slip out of the eye easily, secure the ribbon to the needle by piercing the ribbon about ¼ in. (5 mm) from the cut end using the point of the needle. Holding the tail with your free hand, push the needle through to form a knot at the eye.

STARTING/ENDING RIBBON (2)

Make a small knot at the end of the ribbon to start. To end ribbons, either make a knot or secure to the back of the fabric with tiny stitches using a fine needle and thread that matches your fabric.

1

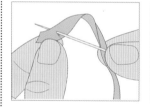

2

Finishing

Once you have completed the embroidery, be sure to take the time to block and press your work to remove markings and creases and set the stitches.

BLOCKING

If your work fits entirely within a hoop or a frame and the fabric is still taut, leave it there and dampen it using a spray bottle set on mist. For water-soluble markings that remain, lightly brush over them with a wet cotton swab to remove. Leave until almost dry.

If your work doesn't fit fully in a frame or has become loose or distorted, remove the work from the hoop or frame and pin it onto an ironing board, making sure that

it is lightly stretched and the grain of the fabric is straight. With a spray bottle set on mist, dampen your work. Leave until almost dry.

PRESSING

After the embroidery has been blocked and is almost dry, give your work a quick press with an iron. Lay the work face down on a padded surface, such as three or four layers of a folded towel. Heat the iron to a setting suitable for both fabric and threads. Where several settings apply, choose the lowest. If necessary, dampen a lightweight cloth and place over the embroidery when pressing to lightly steam. Iron the back of the work only. Do not press ribbon embroidery.

Techniques

Interfacing

Fabric that is being embroidered for a project sometimes requires additional thickness and body, which can be achieved by adding a second layer of cloth to support and stabilize it. It also serves to reduce puckering and distortion, and prevent fabric from fraying.

APPLYING INTERFACING

Interfacing is available in a variety of weights and types, but for embroidery, lightweight grade, woven interfacing is best. Anything heavier will make it harder to pass the needle through the fabric and cause the threads to wear faster. Because heat can cause the ink from dressmaker's carbon to set permanently, only mark the fabric after the interfacing has been attached and the fabric is completely cool.

Start by ironing (follow the manufacturer's instructions) in the center and work out to each side, lifting the iron and setting it down each time instead of sliding, as this may cause the interfacing to shift.

Appliqué

Appliqué is the technique of attaching fabric shapes onto a background of another fabric. Such shapes may be stitched on using tiny matching stitches or with decorative embroidery stitches.

The technique provides a quick and simple way of achieving bold, dramatic effects. Almost any fabric may be appliquéd, but stretch fabrics are best avoided, as are coarsely woven fabrics that are liable to fray. To make the work easy to handle, choose fabrics that are closely woven and of similar weight.

Appliqué is a great way of achieving a bold contrast to the background fabric.

APPLYING FUSIBLE WEBBING

Fusible webbing is a web of heat-sensitive fiber backed with greaseproof paper used to attach the appliqué shape to the background. It does away with the need to completely cover the raw edges of the motifs with stitching as it prevents fraying.

1 Copy the pattern in reverse on the paper side of the fusible webbing.
2 Attach fusible webbing to the wrong side of the appliqué fabric.
3 Cut out the appliqué piece and remove the paper from the fusible webbing.
4 With the fusible webbing facing down on the right side of the base fabric, attach the appliqué piece. Add embroidery stitches.

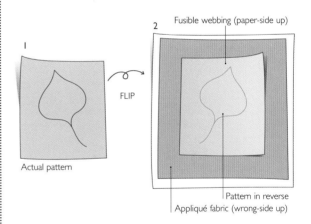

1
Actual pattern

FLIP

2
Fusible webbing (paper-side up)
Pattern in reverse
Appliqué fabric (wrong-side up)

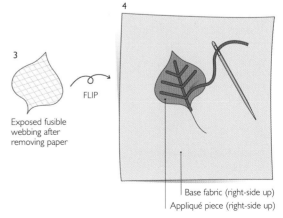

3
Exposed fusible webbing after removing paper

FLIP

4
Base fabric (right-side up)
Appliqué piece (right-side up)

Dimensional work

PADDING WITH FELT OR FILLING

To pad a motif, use felt or filling material. With filling, the embroidery is created on a separate fabric cut to shape and stuffed with filling as it is stitched in place (1). With felt, the stitches are made directly over the felt to cover (2).

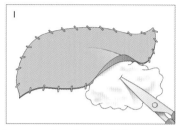

Leave a small gap through which you can adequately stuff your motif.

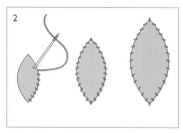

Begin with a small piece of felt and stitch larger ones over the top to create a dimensional piece.

GATHERING FABRIC TO CREATE A 3-D EFFECT

1 Embroider your motif. Make a row of running stitch around the motif about ⅛ in. (3 mm) from the edge of the stitching, leaving the thread ends free.

2 Cut out the motif with about ¼ in. (7 mm) seam allowance, then pull the running stitch thread to gather the seam allowance to the back of the stitching (a). Secure the fabric (b).

3 Sew the motif onto the base fabric along the pattern line, leaving a small opening.

4 Stuff the motif with filling, then sew the opening closed. For small pieces, you may find that no filling is necessary, as the fabric gathered to the back of the piece provides enough cushion.

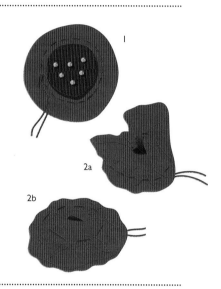

MAKING WIRED PIECES

1 Bend the wire to the pattern form, overlapping the ends of wire slightly. Couch down with one strand of embroidery floss. The ends of the wire are secured with several stitches made right next to each other over the two wire ends.

2 Embroider according to the stitching directions.

3 Cut out with a ⅛-in. (3-mm) margin all around. Cut slits in the margin, if necessary, to take away bulk.

4 Using fabric glue, secure the fabric to the back of the piece.

5 Sew down according to the motif pattern.

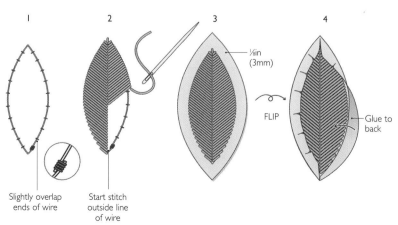

Slightly overlap ends of wire

Start stitch outside line of wire

⅛in (3mm)

FLIP

Glue to back

STUMPWORK BERRIES

1 Thread one strand of embroidery floss onto a blunt-tipped needle like a cross stitch needle. Leaving a 4 in. (10 cm) tail, take the needle up through the bead.

2 Bring the thread down outside the bead, then take the needle up through the bead again. Repeat the process, wrapping the bead until it is completely covered. End the threads when you have about 4 in. (10 cm) left on the needle, taking the needle down through the hole and catching the threads in the hole to secure. Start new threads at the bottom, as before.

3 After you make the final wrap, pass the thread through a seed bead, then down through the wrapped bead. Do this one more time and finish with the thread at the bottom with the other loose threads.

4 Pass the remaining threads to the back of the base fabric and secure the bead and loose ends.

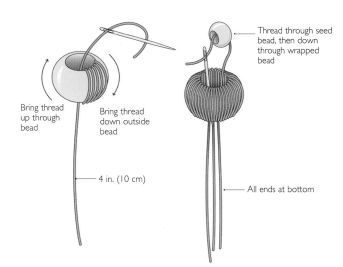

Bring thread up through bead

Bring thread down outside bead

4 in. (10 cm)

Thread through seed bead, then down through wrapped bead

All ends at bottom

STANDING BEADS

1 Bring the thread up to the front of the work where you want the standing beads. Thread as many beads as specified.

2 Skipping the last bead that was threaded, go back through the rest of the beads to the back of the fabric.

3 Come up through the fabric where you want the next standing beads and repeat from step 1.

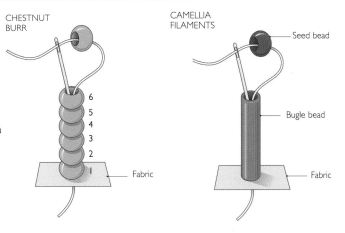

CHESTNUT BURR

6
5
4
3
2
1

Fabric

CAMELLIA FILAMENTS

Seed bead

Bugle bead

Fabric

Stitch directory

This section will show you how to form all the stitches that are used to make the motifs in this book. Each stitch is described with instructions and diagrams, with examples of the stitch from the motifs to demonstrate how it can be applied.

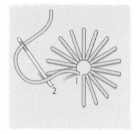
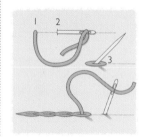
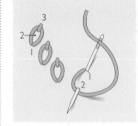

STRAIGHT STITCH
Work in any direction:
Bring the needle up at 1 and insert it at 2. Repeat as required.
Where several straight stitches are closely grouped, it is best to work them all in a similar direction, e.g. from bottom to top, or from top to bottom.

SPLIT STITCH
Work from left to right:
Bring the needle up at 1 and down at 2. Pull through firmly. Bring the needle up again at 3, through the center of the thread. Repeat as required.

LAZY DAISY STITCH
Work in any direction:
Bring the needle up at 1 and insert it at the same place, leaving a loop of thread on the surface. Bring the needle up at 2, inside the loop, and down at 3, outside the loop, making a tiny stitch to hold the loop in place. Repeat as required.
For a longer tail, point 3 may be some distance away from point 2.

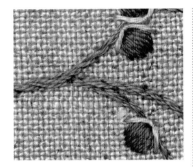

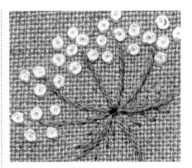

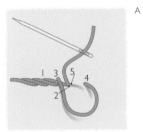

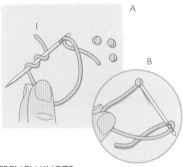

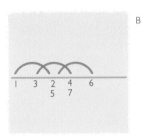

WHIPPED STEM STITCH

Work from left to right or top to bottom:

Make a line of stem stitch (see left). Bring the needle up at 1 and switch to a blunt needle. Pass the needle from right to left under the point where the stitches overlap, without piercing the fabric (2 and 3). Pass the needle to the wrong side at the center top of the last stem stitch.

FRENCH KNOTS

Work in any direction:

Fig A Bring the needle up at 1. Holding the thread taut with the finger and thumb of your left hand, wind the thread once or twice (not more) quite tightly around the needle tip.

Fig B Still holding the thread, insert the needle very close to point 1 and pull the needle through to the back of the work so the twists lie neatly on the fabric surface. Repeat as required.

STEM STITCH

Work from left to right:

Fig A Bring the needle up at 1, down at 2, and up at 3, halfway between 1 and 2, above the thread, then down at 4 and next to 2, above the stitch. Repeat to the end of the line. Each stitch should be the same length and begin halfway along the previous stitch.

Fig B For a finer line, take the needle down directly on the pattern line at 4 and up right at 2, so that the stitches are worked directly on the required line.

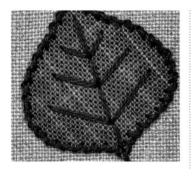

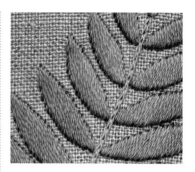

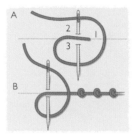

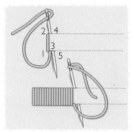

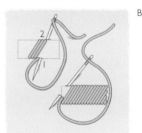

TWISTED CHAIN STITCH

Work from top to bottom:

Fig A Bring the needle up at 1 and down at 2, a little below and to the left of 1. Looping the thread as shown, bring the needle up again at 3.

Fig B Take the needle down at 4, outside the previous loop, twist the thread as before, and bring the needle up at 5. Repeat as required. Fasten off the last loop with a small stitch, as for chain stitch.

CORAL STITCH

Work from right to left:

Fig A Bring the needle up at 1, lay the thread along the line to the left. Take a small vertical stitch across the line from 2 to 3, with the thread looped as shown. Pull through to form a small knot.

Fig B Repeat, spacing the knots as desired. Fasten off by inserting the needle just outside the last knot. When working rows close together as a filling, fit the knots into spaces between the knots of the previous row.

STRAIGHT SATIN STITCH

Work from left to right:

Fig A Bring the needle up at 1, down at 2, up at 3, down at 4, and up at 5. Repeat as required. Stitches should be close together, with no fabric showing between them.

SLANTED SATIN STITCH

Choose the direction of the slant to suit the shape: stitches that are too long will not keep their shape. Stitches on different areas may be worked in different directions to catch the light.

Fig B Begin at the center of the shape: bring the needle up at 1 and down at 2. The first stitch sets the slant for all subsequent stitches. Work parallel stitches from the center out to the right. Then return to the center and work parallel stitches out to the left.

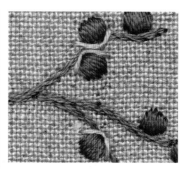

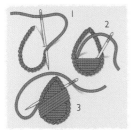

A

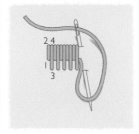

A

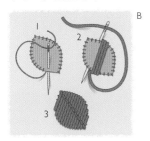

B

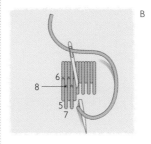

B

FLY STITCH

Work in any direction:
Bring the needle up at 1 and down at 2, leaving a loop of thread. Bring the needle up at 3, inside the loop, and down at 4, outside the loop, holding the loop in place with a small stitch. Repeat as required. For a longer tail, point 4 may be some distance below point 3.

PADDED SATIN STITCH
Padded with stitches

Decide in which direction the final layer of stitches will slant.
Fig A Outline the shape with split stitch (1). Cover the area with satin stitch (left), slanting the stitches in the opposite direction to that required for the final layer, stitching just outside the split stitch outline (2). Work the final layer of satin stitch, slanting as required (3).

Padded with felt

Cut the shape from color-fast felt.
Fig B Using a single strand of floss, stitch the felt in position with small, straight stitches placed across the raw edges (1). Cover the shape with satin stitch (2). Details may be added by working a line of small backstitch to tie down the satin stitches (3).

LONG AND SHORT SATIN STITCH

Start from the center of the form and work out to each side:
Fig A Begin at the top with a row of long and short stitches: bring the needle up at 1, down at 2, up at 3, and down at 4. Repeat to the right.
Fig B For the second row, bring the needle up at 5, down at 6, piercing the base of the short stitch above, up at 7, and down at 8, piercing the base of the long stitch above. Repeat to the right. Repeat this row. End with a row of long and short stitches at the lower edge.

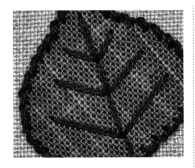

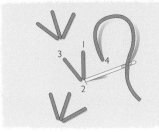

FERN STITCH

Work in any direction:
Bring the needle up at 1 and down at 2
to make the center stitch in the required
direction. Bring the needle up at 3, down
at 2, up at 4, and down again at 2.
Repeat as required.
The three stitches in each group may be
all the same length, with equal angles
between them, or they may be varied as
required for foliage effects.

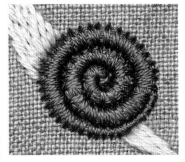

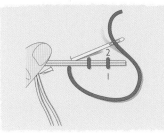

A

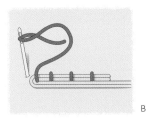

B

COUCHING LINES

Work in any direction:
Fig A Bring the laid thread up at the end
of the pattern line. Bring the tying thread
up at 1. Hold the laid thread in place
with your left thumb and insert the
needle at 2, making a small vertical tying
stitch. Repeat at regular intervals along
the line. To create satin couching, make
the tying stitches right next to each other
so there are no spaces in between.

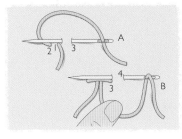

GHIORDES KNOT STITCH

Working from left to right:
Fig A Insert the needle at 1, leaving a
short tail on the surface. Hold down the
tail with your left thumb, bring the
needle up at 2 and down at 3, with the
thread looped above, as shown. Bring
the needle out again at 1.
Fig B Pull through firmly. Form a loop
as shown and insert the needle at 4 to
begin the next repeat by bringing the
needle up again at 3. Repeat to the right.
At the end of the row, cut the thread,
leaving a short tail. Return to the left to
begin the next row. Work the next row
one thread above the first row. Repeat as
required. After completion, cut and trim
the loops if required. When filling a
circular form, work the stitch in a spiral
from the outside in.

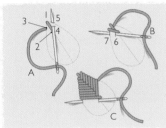

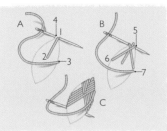

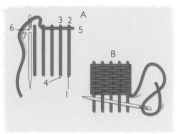

FISHBONE STITCH

Work from tip of shape to base:

Fig A Bring the needle up at 1 and down at 2, up again at 3, and down at 4, just overlapping the previous stitch. Bring the needle up at 5.

Fig B Insert the needle at 6, just overlapping the previous stitch and bring it up at 7 to begin the next pair of stitches.

Fig C Continue making stitches alternately at the left and right, just overlapping along the center line.

RAISED FISHBONE STITCH

Fig A Work from 1 at the top of the motif and make a vertical stitch halfway down to 2, and bring the needle back to the front at 3. Make a small horizontal stitch at the top of the motif, inserting the needle at 4 and bringing it out at 5.

Fig B Make a stitch that enters at 6 and emerges again at 7, right below the stitch at 3. Make another horizontal stitch at the top of the motif, just below the first stitch.

Fig C Repeat these last two steps until the motif is completely filled with stitches. At the end of the line of stitching, take the thread through to the reverse to fasten off.

NEEDLEWEAVING

Fig A Begin by working a series of vertical stitches. Bring the needle up at 1, down at 2, up at 3, and down at 4. Repeat across the whole area.

Using the same or another color and a blunt needle, bring the thread up at 5. Weave the needle over and under the vertical threads and take it down at 6 and up at 7.

Fig B Weave the second journey, alternating "unders" with "overs" of the previous journey and vice versa.

Repeat the two weaving journeys as required.

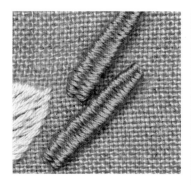

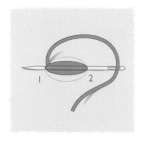

GRANITOS STITCH

Bring the needle up at 1 and down at 2. Repeat, always coming up and going down in the same hole. Continue until the stitch is the desired size.

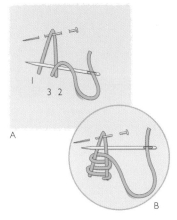

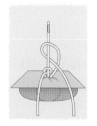

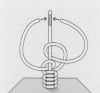

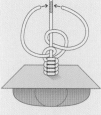

TWO-SPOKE WOVEN PICOT

Fig A Insert a pin at the pointed end of the picot shape required. Bring a blunt needle up at 1, over the pin and down at 2, and up at 3. Instead of a pin, the point can be stitched down with separate thread to be removed later.

Fig B Pass the needle over the right-hand thread and back under it from right to left, without piercing the fabric. On the return journey, pass the needle over the left-hand thread and back under it from left to right, without piercing the fabric. Repeat these two sequences until the shape is full, closely packing the lines of the weaving to completely cover the two vertical threads. Remove the pin and insert the needle back through the fabric at the top point. For a picot that is not sewn down at the tip, work the strands of thread one by one into the back side of the picot, being careful not to distort the woven threads.

DOUBLE DRIZZLE STITCH

Fig A Bring two threads up through the fabric. Unthread the needle. With a pincushion placed behind the fabric, insert the point of the needle between the two threads.

Fig B Create a loop with the left-hand thread as shown and slip the loop onto the needle. Pull the thread to make snug but not tight.

Fig C Next, create a loop with the right-hand thread as shown and slip the loop onto the needle. This loop should be formed in a mirror image to the left-hand loop. Pull the thread to make snug.

Fig D Continue creating loops onto the needle by alternating between the two threads.

Fig E When the desired length has been achieved, thread the needle with both threads from front to back. Remove the pincushion and take the ends down to the back of the fabric.

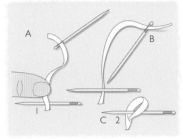

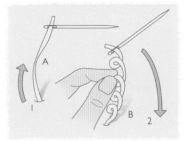

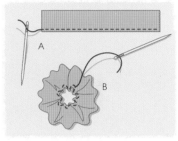

RIBBON STITCH

Fig A Fasten the ribbon at the back. Bring it up at 1 and hold it down flat against the fabric with your thumb. With a spare needle, carefully lift the point of entry.
Fig B Now place the spare needle, horizontally to the ribbon, where the curl is desired.
Fig C Take the needle down at 2, through the ribbon, over the horizontal needle, and through to the back of the fabric. Carefully pull the ribbon through the fabric, making sure you do not pull the curl right through. Fasten the stitch off at the back.

TWISTED STRAIGHT STITCH

Fig A Fasten the ribbon at the back of the fabric. Bring it up at 1, holding it above the fabric with finger and thumb.
Fig B Twist the ribbon once, twice, or several times, depending on the effect required, and hold the twists with finger and thumb. Take the point of the needle down at 2, and fasten the stitch at the back.

GATHERED RIBBON FLOWER

Fig A Using a needle threaded with matching thread, stitch tiny gathering stitches along one edge of the ribbon. (If working with more than one layer of ribbon, pin them together before stitching.)
Fig B Pull the ribbon up until it forms a neat circle. Tucking the raw edges to the back, stitch the two ends of the ribbon together. Stitch the flower into position on the fabric using matching thread.

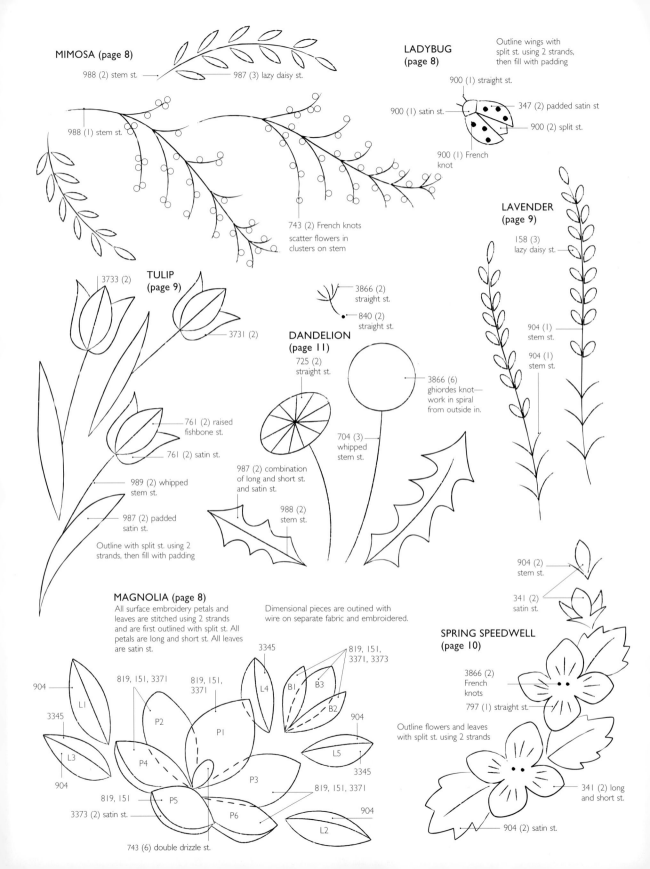

MIMOSA (page 8)

988 (2) stem st.

987 (3) lazy daisy st.

988 (1) stem st.

743 (2) French knots scatter flowers in clusters on stem

LADYBUG (page 8)

Outline wings with split st. using 2 strands, then fill with padding

900 (1) straight st.

900 (1) satin st.

347 (2) padded satin st

900 (2) split st.

900 (1) French knot

LAVENDER (page 9)

158 (3) lazy daisy st.

904 (1) stem st.

904 (1) stem st.

TULIP (page 9)

3733 (2)

3731 (2)

761 (2) raised fishbone st.

761 (2) satin st.

989 (2) whipped stem st.

987 (2) padded satin st.

Outline with split st. using 2 strands, then fill with padding

DANDELION (page 11)

3866 (2) straight st.

840 (2) straight st.

725 (2) straight st.

3866 (6) ghiordes knot—work in spiral from outside in.

704 (3) whipped stem st.

987 (2) combination of long and short st. and satin st.

988 (2) stem st.

904 (2) stem st.

341 (2) satin st.

SPRING SPEEDWELL (page 10)

3866 (2) French knots

797 (1) straight st.

Outline flowers and leaves with split st. using 2 strands

341 (2) long and short st.

904 (2) satin st.

MAGNOLIA (page 8)

All surface embroidery petals and leaves are stitched using 2 strands and are first outlined with split st. All petals are long and short st. All leaves are satin st.

Dimensional pieces are outined with wire on separate fabric and embroidered.

904

L1

3345

L3

904

819, 151, 3371

P2

3345

P4

819, 151

3373 (2) satin st.

P5

743 (6) double drizzle st.

819, 151, 3371

P1

3345

L4

819, 151, 3371, 3373

B1   B3

B2

904

L5

3345

904

L2

819, 151, 3371

P3

P6

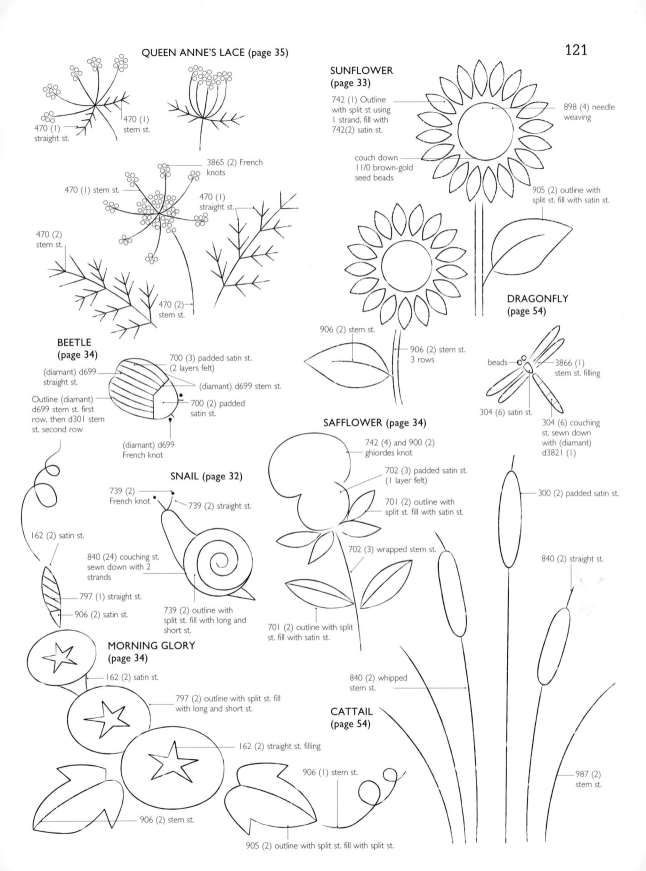

QUEEN ANNE'S LACE (page 35)

470 (1) straight st.

470 (1) stem st.

3865 (2) French knots

470 (1) stem st.

470 (1) straight st.

470 (2) stem st.

470 (2) stem st.

SUNFLOWER (page 33)

742 (1) Outline with split st using 1 strand, fill with 742(2) satin st.

898 (4) needle weaving

couch down 11/0 brown-gold seed beads

905 (2) outline with split st. fill with satin st.

906 (2) stem st.

906 (2) stem st. 3 rows

BEETLE (page 34)

(diamant) d699 straight st.

700 (3) padded satin st. (2 layers felt)

(diamant) d699 stem st.

Outline (diamant) d699 stem st. first row, then d301 stem st. second row

700 (2) padded satin st.

(diamant) d699 French knot

DRAGONFLY (page 54)

beads

3866 (1) stem st. filling

304 (6) satin st.

304 (6) couching st. sewn down with (diamant) d3821 (1)

SAFFLOWER (page 34)

742 (4) and 900 (2) ghiordes knot

702 (3) padded satin st. (1 layer felt)

701 (2) outline with split st. fill with satin st.

300 (2) padded satin st.

702 (3) wrapped stem st.

SNAIL (page 32)

739 (2) French knot

739 (2) straight st.

162 (2) satin st.

840 (24) couching st. sewn down with 2 strands

797 (1) straight st.

906 (2) satin st.

739 (2) outline with split st. fill with long and short st.

701 (2) outline with split st. fill with satin st.

840 (2) straight st.

MORNING GLORY (page 34)

162 (2) satin st.

797 (2) outline with split st. fill with long and short st.

162 (2) straight st. filling

840 (2) whipped stem st.

CATTAIL (page 54)

906 (1) stem st.

987 (2) stem st.

906 (2) stem st.

905 (2) outline with split st. fill with split st.

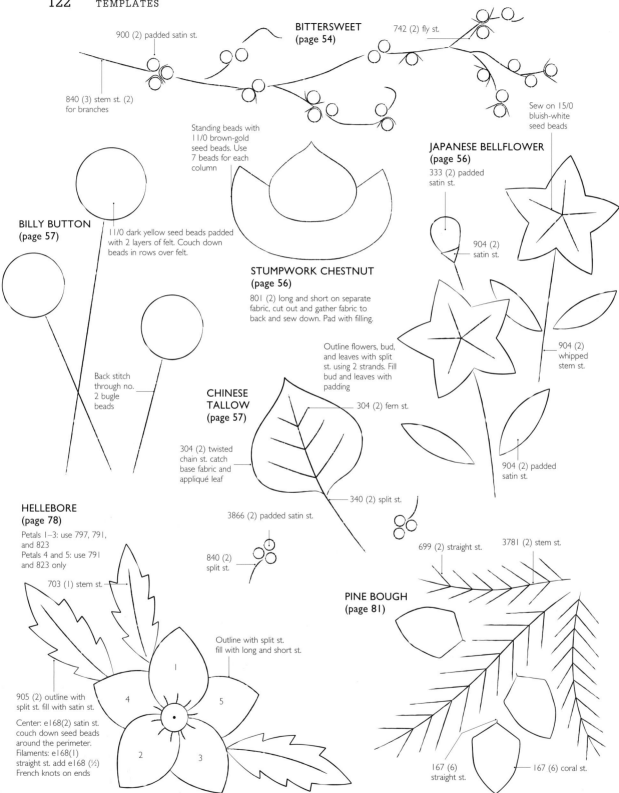

BITTERSWEET
(page 54)

900 (2) padded satin st.

742 (2) fly st.

840 (3) stem st. (2) for branches

Standing beads with 11/0 brown-gold seed beads. Use 7 beads for each column

Sew on 15/0 bluish-white seed beads

JAPANESE BELLFLOWER
(page 56)

333 (2) padded satin st.

904 (2) satin st.

904 (2) whipped stem st.

904 (2) padded satin st.

BILLY BUTTON
(page 57)

11/0 dark yellow seed beads padded with 2 layers of felt. Couch down beads in rows over felt.

STUMPWORK CHESTNUT
(page 56)

801 (2) long and short on separate fabric, cut out and gather fabric to back and sew down. Pad with filling.

Outline flowers, bud, and leaves with split st. using 2 strands. Fill bud and leaves with padding

Back stitch through no. 2 bugle beads

304 (2) fern st.

CHINESE TALLOW
(page 57)

304 (2) twisted chain st. catch base fabric and appliqué leaf

340 (2) split st.

3866 (2) padded satin st.

HELLEBORE
(page 78)

Petals 1–3: use 797, 791, and 823
Petals 4 and 5: use 791 and 823 only

840 (2) split st.

699 (2) straight st.

3781 (2) stem st.

703 (1) stem st.

PINE BOUGH
(page 81)

Outline with split st. fill with long and short st.

905 (2) outline with split st. fill with satin st.

Center: e168(2) satin st. couch down seed beads around the perimeter. Filaments: e168(1) straight st. add e168 (½) French knots on ends

1

4   5

2   3

167 (6) straight st.

167 (6) coral st.

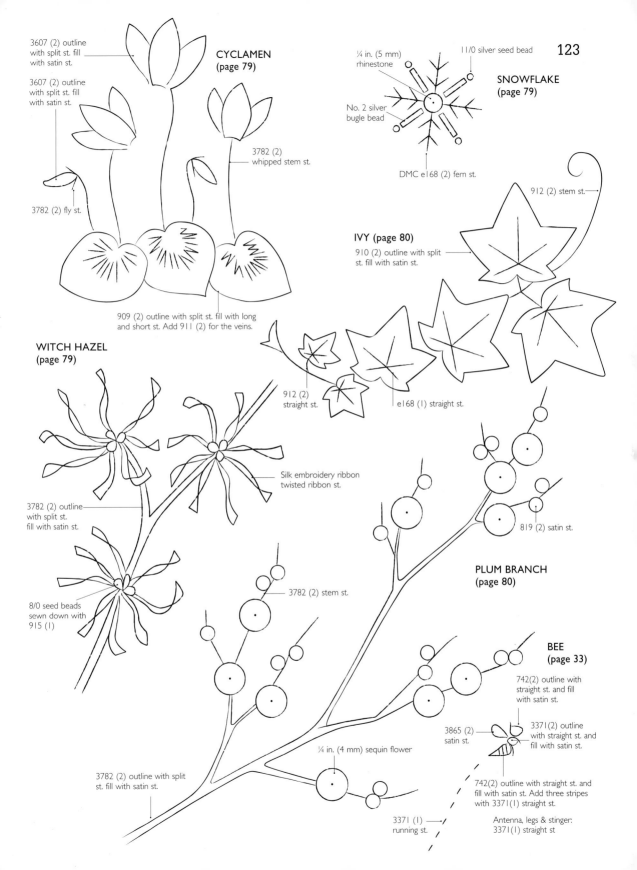

CYCLAMEN
(page 79)

3607 (2) outline with split st. fill with satin st.

3607 (2) outline with split st. fill with satin st.

3782 (2) whipped stem st.

3782 (2) fly st.

909 (2) outline with split st. fill with long and short st. Add 911 (2) for the veins.

¼ in. (5 mm) rhinestone

11/0 silver seed bead

SNOWFLAKE
(page 79)

No. 2 silver bugle bead

DMC e168 (2) fern st.

912 (2) stem st.

IVY (page 80)

910 (2) outline with split st. fill with satin st.

912 (2) straight st.

e168 (1) straight st.

WITCH HAZEL
(page 79)

Silk embroidery ribbon twisted ribbon st.

3782 (2) outline with split st. fill with satin st.

8/0 seed beads sewn down with 915 (1)

819 (2) satin st.

PLUM BRANCH
(page 80)

3782 (2) stem st.

BEE
(page 33)

742(2) outline with straight st. and fill with satin st.

3865 (2) satin st.

3371(2) outline with straight st. and fill with satin st.

742(2) outline with straight st. and fill with satin st. Add three stripes with 3371(1) straight st.

¼ in. (4 mm) sequin flower

3782 (2) outline with split st. fill with satin st.

3371 (1) running st.

Antenna, legs & stinger: 3371(1) straight st

Fold your fabric in half and place the fold against this dotted line.

Sewing line

Cutting line

DAFFODIL HANGER
COVER PATTERN
(page 24)

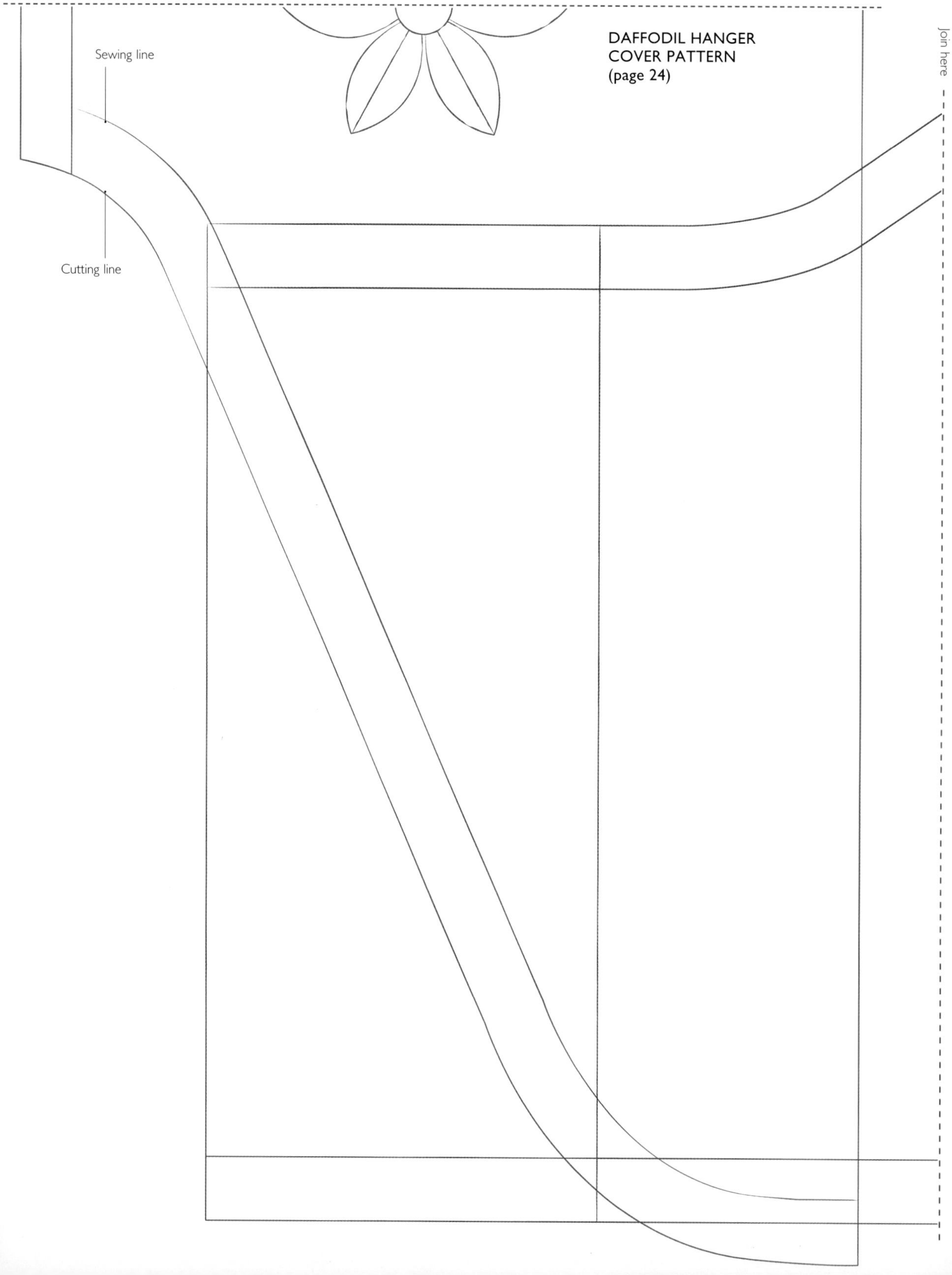

Join here

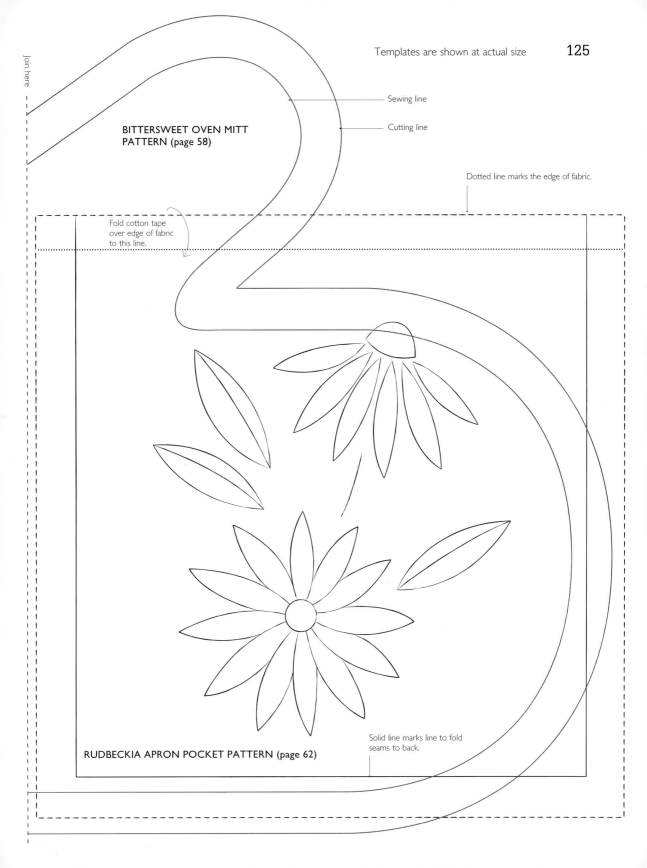

Join here

Sewing line

Cutting line

BITTERSWEET OVEN MITT PATTERN (page 58)

Dotted line marks the edge of fabric.

Fold cotton tape over edge of fabric to this line.

RUDBECKIA APRON POCKET PATTERN (page 62)

Solid line marks line to fold seams to back.

BITTERSWEET OVEN MITT PATTERN PIECES

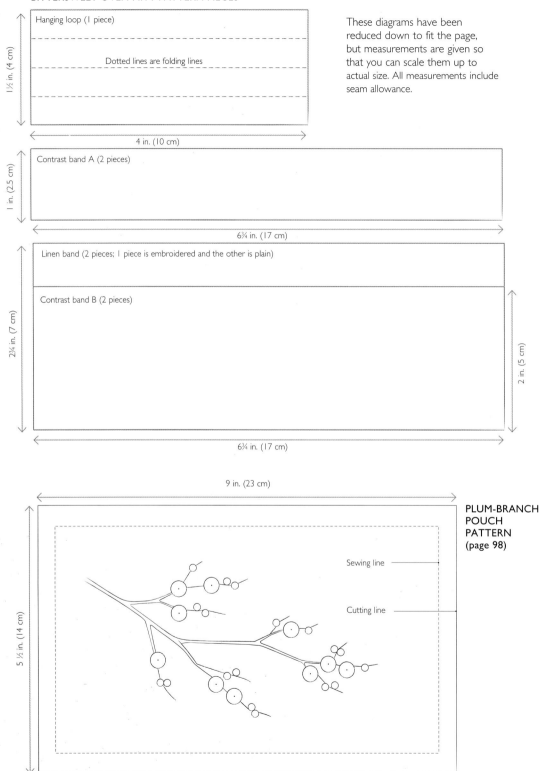

Hanging loop (1 piece)

Dotted lines are folding lines

1½ in. (4 cm)

4 in. (10 cm)

These diagrams have been reduced down to fit the page, but measurements are given so that you can scale them up to actual size. All measurements include seam allowance.

Contrast band A (2 pieces)

1 in. (2.5 cm)

6¾ in. (17 cm)

Linen band (2 pieces; 1 piece is embroidered and the other is plain)

Contrast band B (2 pieces)

2¾ in. (7 cm)

2 in. (5 cm)

6¾ in. (17 cm)

9 in. (23 cm)

PLUM-BRANCH POUCH PATTERN
(page 98)

Sewing line

Cutting line

5 ½ in. (14 cm)

Leave open for turning

Index

Credits

Many thanks to DMC Creative World who generously supplied the embroidery thread used in this book.

AUTHOR ACKNOWLEDGMENTS

Thank you to Quarto for giving me the opportunity to create this book and for bringing everything together in such a beautiful way. A special thank you also to my mother and my son, Alex, for their invaluable input and support.